I0158871

Peace Goddess Spirit of the Field
The Intimacy Sutras

Sunny Jetsun

Love is the Best
Let it go straight into the heart of Someone you Love

Art by T. Bird a pseudonym of Sunny Jetsun

All names, characters, and incidents portrayed in this book are fictitious. No identification with actual persons, is intended or should be inferred.

Copyright Disclaimer ~ Under Section 107 of 1976 Copyright Act, allowance is made of 'fair use' for purposes of knowledge. The moral right of the author has been asserted 2016

Copyright © 2016 Sunny Jetsun
All rights reserved.
978-1-910363-31-7

Peace Goddess*Spirit of the Field*The Intimacy Sutras

Sunny Jetsun

<u>**Other Books by Sunny Jetsun**</u>
'Driving My Scooter Through The Asteroid Field
Coming Down Over Venus ~ Hallo Baba'
'Light love Angels from Heaven. New Generation,
Inspiration, Revolution, Revelation ~
All the Colours of Cosmic Rainbows'
'Green Eve * Don't lose the Light Vortex *
My brain's gone on holiday ~ free flowing feelings'
'Surfing or Suffering together * Sense Consciousness
fields of a body with streams and stars of hearts'
'When You're happy you got wings on your back ~
Reposez vos oreilles a Goa; We're only one kiss away'
'PSYCHIC PSYCHEDELIC'
'Streaming Lemon Topaz Sunbeams'
'Invasion of Beauty *FLASH * The Love Mudras'
'Patchouli Showers ~ Tantric Temples'
'It's Just a Story* We Are All The Sun* Sweet Surrender'
Anthology #1 ~ 'Enjoy The Revolution'
Anthology # 2 ~ 'Love & Freedom ~ Welcome'
'He Lives In A Parallel Universe'
'Queen of Space King of Flower Power dripping Rainbows'
'All Love Frequency ~ In Zero Space'
'Heavenly Bodies ~ Celestial Alignments*
Feeling ~ Energy that Is LOVE in Itself'
'I've been to Venus & back*These Are Real Feelings*
Let the Universe Guide Your Heart * through Space'
* The Kiss in Slaughterhouse 6 *

<u>UPPER</u>

No one caring about anyone else.
He used to believe in the Universe
then he stopped! The Robbing Hood.
"I was the happiest guy in the queue!"
Why am I still here, I should be dead?
I told you many times how I felt you took no notice, now I'm gone.
Thing is to get on with it and be happy ~ it's the way you look at it.
No Structure duality of the Lover & the beloved, be as one energy.
Live in resonant harmony with nature not destroying her essence!
Pissing on the flower, it's withering, dying, no smile inside, dead!
Are you committed to me Baby? It's not even a love affair now!
Not going to the parties, tuning into beautiful psychedelic music.
"These people make me dance"
*

<u>Establishment Headlines.</u>

Brainwashing <:> written in Tablets of Stone.
They might hear it but will they f.... believe it?
None of it reported in the Newspapers or on TV.
The Blueprint for what people were going to Think.
A Government whitewash, didn't even do an autopsy!
The bombs came from underneath the derailed carriage,
blown up off the rails! Was Building 7 collapsing or not?
"The BBC. is Lying to you, not telling us the whole Truth"
The gears of the machine rigged for this to happen.
Saying anything to fuck up the program and you will die!
It's usually what's not in the Media that's the most important;
Not about a Beauty Queen from Brazil winning Miss Universe.

<u>Another Victim of Duality</u>
If you want to get into that mindset of being guilty for smoking
tobacco in a joint! Giving up this deception, worldly delusion.
This entity loves pain, more, more, more, more, more ~
Forget the unconscious story transmute its feeling.
A blessing in disguise, can it bear it any longer?
Love & empathy the highest level of intelligence.
Abstraction all in it together ~ crossing a sizzling bed of fire.
That's not God it's a picture of God but he has memory loss.

*

<u>Keep it True.</u>
"Are you a Nazi,
I never met one before,
can I touch you?"
Visiting the scraped skull room!
Dark with a pile of bones and heads.
What do you do with all those bodies?
What kind of human beings are they?
Need to bring up our frequency together!

*

<u>Of Us All</u>
"Not a Spiritual bone in his body!"
He can't get close and open his feelings;
Don't wanna do that! Free to do what you want.
Hopefully makes you happy letting the addiction to pain go.
Like a dog with three dicks and a bag of Poppers!
He believes in God but he's not religious!
Ultimately it's all changing ~ for everyone.
"Makes you feel very light when you got nothing"

2

<u>Buy a dog a pizza.</u>
LOVE IS THE BEST.
The Devil is at work deep inside the Vatican!
All is lost, 'the dark night of the soul' a cardinal belief.
Natural flow of light ~ You both get the Pleasure!
Being in that Cosmic Space.

*

<u>Holy Fools</u>
Love is happening of its own accord ~
Any reason why dark Psy*trance is shit?
Trishul of Shiva ~ "I'm so imminent!" OK...
"Yes he does coke but not with you!" Star*chasm.
That's where we work out our politics
on the dance floor!
We're Shiva People.

*

<u>FLOWER POWER</u>
Resonating ~ always coming from omnipresent chakras,
can you feel me dancing in there? "Blessing my Life"
'See yourself as a bio*org * multi*dimensional being'
"So you can see you can be it ~ You are already It!"
Sit in the back of the Limousine and enjoy the ride.
"I didn't do anything ~ it just happened."
The more enlightened the dark has to go.
Pure Intelligence ~ Pure Feeling
Pure Conscious * Infinite Energy.
"I've had enough of suffering!"
Her mind was demanding a lot!
You have to know what you want
or what you don't want Baby!

Clean as you go
Gotta do it to know it ~
"What's the best for YOU mate?"
"Most friends take drugs in my circle"
There's nothing in there for a bad trip
unless you got a messy head ~ be balance.
The more you do the easier it gets.
Nothing else rattlin' around ~
Except for your Sweetness
*

Time to say goodbye
I'm more for the feelin' than the meanin' ~
I realized that her feelings changed so quickly!
Destiny! The Empress' new cuntipotent had a brainwave.
"Are we goin' to have dead radiated humans everywhere?"
You don't want to wake up with a woman covered in blood!
Authority wants to keep you in a box to control all of you!
Sex, drugs, rock and roll and killing people via a drone
*

Cold Turkey Breaking Bondage
The one who is dumped, unaware that moment is coming ~
very soon from around the corner with a smile or a hatchet!
That one is in the position of still being in Love but the object
of that attention has changed her makeup and feelings like a
Probe from Venus! Need to realize that vibe has gone even when
the object is lying naked next to you or left ~ that love changed.
Wanting possession of that hot luscious memory or let it be free.
Time to decimate all those feelings or let them fly to Heaven.
It's all Vibration

OM TOTEM

You weren't there channeling Zen ~
'There's Nothing New Under the Sun'
Try the sound of one hand clapping mate.
Synergy, Spontaneity ~ Love's in super Action.
Wolf's Tao card ~ Awareness no personal volition.
Staying outside keeping the sheep shitting together.
Got no enemies, everyone gets a wakeup call.
You find what's Inside, choice about Me not about You.
Life is always looking for new ways to express itself.
Practicing being Mindful of everything you do.
All kinds of Oracles lying around everywhere!
Eagles rising high above the 'Quack Quack'
Spread your angel wings, responding to flying.
Landing and becoming the 'Me' again.

*

Organic Unity the Human Race

You won't know until you're there ~
In the right spot of the Intuitive river.
Venus put you here, none of my business.
Life has an agenda; You love the Planet right?
It's in our own head ~ 'Me'
The Perfect World

*

The Disunity of the Human Spirit

Oneness with the Supreme ~ nothing else is Real.
Only the Divine and nothing more.
Still seeing everyone as different!
Looking on same same Universe ~
"Om Namah Shivaya"

Stick to your guns!
Keep your eye on the ball ~ If there's a queue I don't need it!
There is no evolution context, they lied ~ just Transcendence.
The establishment are running the show, setting Their Rules.
He never said we came from Aliens just far beyond any galaxy.
Still thinking about it ~ when it gets clearer you feel it.
Everything that happens around us happens in us.

*

The Fear of God ~ Confessing every action!
The Vatican Mafia ~ "I think I went in the Gas Chamber!"
Yeah if Marbella was so great why the f… come to India?
They're looking for a new place to fuck; 'Sari Up' dancing!
That was his experience who knows what that's about?
"I hate the human f…. race." That's too profound, no?
I don't believe in the end of the World but a Positive Vision.
Smoking THC dope opened my mind and raised my awareness.
Jesus was a rebel who wanted freedom.
The bodiless Spirit of the Bodhi tree.
Religion Stops a lot of wildness!
It's your ego do what you can.
Politics blocks the energy ~
You are where you want to be.
To be Free.

*

Upside down Vision
Flipping hemispheres of creativity ~ reversal of what you want
into a new field*imagination making a positive from a negative.
Chilling out with a Russian, sharing a chillum "Perestroika, da!"

Too Tricksy

"You can fight the darkness or you can light a candle"
"I don't know how I feel about anything anymore"
Lost in the same vast sea looking for each other ~
You go into Consciously or does Consciously come to you?
The more nothing you can do, the stronger it gets.
Aligning me in the moment ~ It just happens, true love.
Love is not crazy, lazy ~ Active Feelings, sharing it.
You believe it, open channel that makes you happy.
Light rays falling on a leaf from a parallel dimension.
Give up your bondage by being in the present.

*

Popcorn Mufti.

I talk so much shit, prancing round the holy yard.
"I'm good because I'm me" ~ wearing conceit well!
Whatever life gives you, it's for you. "It's nice in you here"
Go into the shadows to see the auras ~ raising vibrations.
Can't cope with the adoration ~ culling a sweetheart's clit!
Why is there so much negative Propaganda about Muslims?
#8 Majjid street, 'Inshallah' with a bit of luck, God willing.

*

Energetic Meditation

"The most spiritual thing is to laugh" Ha Ha Ha!
Full on all the time ~ telepathic with E T. dolphins.
Alien eels if you catch them they'll bite your hand off!
I agree we are all nature's Gods, the same quality to be ~
They got married in a prison, all their friends were locked up!
He just loves getting mangled, all smashed up, wobblin' about!
"We're only three meals away from anarchy!"

All Charas

It comes from the most holiest places in the World.
Those spending their life going round beautiful sites.
"Isn't the Planet a wonderful Space and it's our home!"
Shouting from his throne, "Bring the Chief Pharmacist!"
Making a prescryption for an Industrial Ketamine user.
'Extreme pleasure' ~ you'll get a come down from that!
Falling in lust with the Trauma, fully conditioned Love.

*

All the Freedoms You Have!

You can have some very good ~ negative conversions!
The Art is not the artist, it's what is being channeled.
If it comes from the heart it should become a Sutra.
Your Diva cells not demented from Pandora's box.
You got money, eat good food, you'll last longer.
"If it don't bark, it ain't no good mate"
Just a feeding machine!

*

Meister Hofmann's 1200 mikes.

Everything is in Perfection as soon as our hard drive's dross,
conditionings, judgments, labelling, Identificationing, laws;
Authority's rules boxing it off ~ We realise and let them go.
350 micro gms; Overdone it! Keeping the simplicity of life.
"You're never f....... goin' back!" ~ You know what I mean?
We're five+ satellite dishes on Cosmic photon spaceships.
Still trippin' forever in multi * dimensional * Chapora!
No comin' back to this plasma reality ~
talkin' to holograms ~ Full on.
Pure Crystal songlines to Infinity.

<u>OK being Used but not Abused!</u>
In the 'happy to see you smile!' Not pissed off!
"It's all in the LOVE ~ Moon dance Absolutely,
making a delightful cuppa coffee in the morning"
Resenting it, you think it's only another f... chore
and you don't wanna do it for me darling! Simple.

*

<u>Organic India?</u>
Silent orgasms, hiding the Goddess behind a sheet with a glory hole!
"Selling them dreams of alcohol abuse & Coke the real thing!"
When there is no time to become Love ~
I won't forget your orgasmically blissful lips.
Manifesting Cosmic erections in wet Yonis!
"You gotta stay in Love with it all"
"We're told we're not the Love"
"tell 'em that's all bollocks!"
Looking for the Love ~
We Are the Love.

*

<u>'Classic Literacy'</u>
'The Adam & Eve Story' ~ Evelution
every dot has a reason to be there ~
The same High! That holiday vibe...
'So covert nobody knows what's goin' on!'
The separation of you from the one you love.
Enter disappointment, sorrow and all the angels cried.
Spiritual words decrypted ~
Let's Celebrate with Krishna
singing and dancing to Heaven.

Dropping out the sky!
Newton just made a little formula for Gravity ~
People knew things were falling on the ground!
Going on all the time ~ in the apple orchard.
"I'm addicted to purring pussycats in heat"
All Freedoms you have in rainbow prisms of light.
Timothy Leary's genes tripping in space looking
for X E T. Intelligence ~ enjoying Cosmic flight.

*

Onto the Next One!
Who's biggest producer of Weapons on the Planet?
!!!WEAPONS TO PROTECT YOUR FREEDOM!!!
Mikhail Kalashnikov, Hero, AK-47 inventor dies at 94!
Biggest vested interests in scaring us all to Death!
There's a Crocodile in the pond scavenging for God.
"We're stuck here with a case of stuffed animals!"
"Everything will be alright in the End"

*

Saint or Sinner ~ Itchy Nuclear Killer Reaction!
All the nurses melted on their way back rushing to A&E!
"Kingdom of Heaven is open to all, dropped a 1 Megaton"
Controlling how people think, producing constant crap
for the masses. They're really, really taking the Piss!
Got banged up forever for telling the Truth me Lud.
We find these revelations to be 'Subversive Activity!'
Subtitled but really good, "I expected a Thank You"
Inbred as fuck, if you're a fascist you get into it!
Thinking makes heavier worrying and breathing.

Automatic Death's Drones
"No one left to kill!" "Repeat, over" Can we go home now?
200 million liters of sewrage pumped into the Ganges daily!
Transformation ~ dawn's energy ~ pure in essence.
They were singing from the heart ~
You are feeling when falling in Love
with Divine celestial space.

*

LUSH DUDE
Letting paranoia run wild to control us; Easy Mr!
All the hallucinatory, psychedelic elements gone ~
Oh look! "My brain thinks in a multitude of rays"
"I love that turquoise, crystal clear water"

*

ctrl, alt, delete, reboot
"Can't take sides ~ they're as bad as each other!"
"I'm not in this Elite so I won't be goin' there"
"It's hard to get out of habit, addiction"
Being in the moment ~ No projections.
Not everybody does tomorrow.

*

No Trust Anymore!
Always believed the love would come back ~
How could you not want more of that bliss? ~ Evaporated!
"I got married because my ex-wife wanted to get married"
"Always more room to really fuck up!"
"Like an angel pissing on your tongue"
"You gotta Respect these chicks"
Keeping it Surreal mate!

Still in Love

"I'm at home why not stop by for more blissful kisses?"
Changed reality for another perception inside their dream.
Feeling I am a different being lying naked next to you,
wanting you to touch me deeply in my heart.
Taken for granted because I still adore you.
I came back to carry on kissing your smile.
Ask me anything you want ~
forgot how to give in return.
Lost the passion, desire energy.
Now we've become a lovely memory.
His Image held it together.

*

Only Pepper if Hot

"Take him out and his diabetic neighbour!"
"Bought her a Bindi tracking device for Divalli"
"Kiss my arse we're for you!" Scary as fuck!
Who Cares? Russian chicks every time ~
"They're just F... hot, even unhot ones are hot!"
"Is that injection enough or do you want more?"
"UK dentists think you're a junkie if you want more!"

*

Shamanic not Satanic

I made her Aware of that Monkey Mind.
"She has taught me Patience that's one thing; I did put up with it!"
Mind Working Out in the Front Seat ~ Waiting for a picture.
Not getting into this bat & ball game with you.
It will take us down if you stay there....
I want to Live in Harmony.

Molecular * Procreation
SAVE THE AMAZON ~ SAVE YOUR BREATH!
Accept the other person for who you are ~ sharing the air.
FEELING YOUR HEART ~ not the judging, dualled Mind.
Woman is the Selector ~ spreading her genetic attraction.
Forgiveness, Acceptance Is Transcendence.
You cannot be an Artist and not F E E L
Krishna's dance of Love.

*

Shakti Kali Shanti
'Fear & Loathing in GOA' ~ Unrepresentative Government!
Giving ~ resonating peace vibrations with a Russell Viper.
"I can honestly say that "I never joined the rat race"
"I'm looking for the Cosmic patterns to everything"
Met Venus' twin sister ~ we make our own Heaven.
It's all very beautiful.

*

Globalised Sand Mafias!
Conceptualising disease of Western man and woman.
Diabolical Corporatocracy ~ Your Profits at ANY cost!
The Enlightenment of the Earth, darkness before dawn.
They're going to make it illegal to replant your seeds.
Conglomerations, their shareholders, investors, Directors.
You are behaving diabolically, inhumanely, unnaturally.
What happened to Tony Blair and cronies who sold their souls?
Someone has to stand up for the light, for humanity, for truth.
Thanks to the Dalai Lama, Chelsea Manning, Edward Snowden.
All hail Democracy ~ shit stirring on a Factory Farm!
All hail Truthsayers deserving the Noble Peace Prize!

'Dave my sacred cow'
The rednecks are coming, they've run out of beer!
Biodynamic Acid testament, temptations you like.
Who's your Cacao dealer? ~ It's the Mind Dictator!
"It helps to be bonkers!" Av' a word with yourself.
There's No 'I am' ~ when you drop the obvious lie.
An enlightened man – You can't get enlightened!
*

Diasporatedists
Another ~ 'Slave nation to money'
They wanna rule the Whole World!
All for them to exploit ~ each crumb!
Choice ~ I wanna be in the 'Real World'
We all have to move up somewhere ~
"I can't be different than I truly Am"
*

'The sheep go to church on Sunday
like children with their Teddy bears'
Some people are good carpenters ~
they can make a good dovetail joint.
Man ate Magical mushroom spores from Space,
we came down out the trees; You lost it, Yeah!
Lost your memory of the stoned furry freak tribe!
Evolutionary ~ There is No beginning or ending ~
Cosmic reflections beaming into your changing Space.
Cumulative, leaving behind seeds, genes of blessings.
No enlightenment just Programmed, processing ~
of children of the Divine ~ Receiving Indigo rays!

Absolutely Fantastic
Don't want Isms, you want Wasisms, futurisms,
Orgasisms get over it dude! Standing in the light.
"The only Truth is that you exist, you're Aware &
like it; Seeing it another way ~ Just existence itself.
Life is wonderful ~ when you don't have Opinions!
She hasn't found herself, her happiness ~ a grimace!
That's what she took with her into the Cosmic Ocean.

*

Amazing Nonsense.
"There is no You who is alive there's only Life itself"
Flowing through Form and You ~ growing it as it is.
Not True there's No Self-enquiry ~ Truth is Self-evident.
They're just looking for Desire & Aversion polarity!
Unfolding their Identities from the moment of Birth.
You think you are YOU and YOU will die!
'You're there to heal others not throw stones'
Your energies are scattered ~ Remain Centred!

*

The Universe Makes It Happen
You see the Common sense, I'm not asking
you to believe, to show me Proof ~ without
doubt you cannot grow; What say you Socrates?
Religion you're not allowed doubt or healthy confusion.
It's common sense don't need to exercise any Opinion.
There is No One ~ to have a judgment… Really?
Just the Knower knowing the known > I * AM.
Just a Program running, you're caught up in it or
You're Aware of it ~ There is NO You! Absolutely
Awareness ~ Automatic Attention, Intention
going with the Cosmic flow ~ not side to side

<u>Cosmic Oceanic</u>
"I became Krishna Consciousness ~
"God created Space wo/men ~ Space wo/men made us!"
Krishna's into it all ~ Making the most of every party!
"I'm just gonna have it freestyle ~"
'DNR ' ~ Do not resuscitate your mum!
Doing it, no blocks, resistances, veils,
hidden treasures, top secrets, lost tribes,
vague memories, forbidden desires, taboos, glories.
Swimming in an Open pool of infiniteness ~ Nature.
300 tonnes of radioactive waste dumped into the sea
at TEPCO Fukushima every day, heading your way Baby!
You gotta survive in the arid desert, looking at stars, feeling
windy, moist breeze, wetness over tingling sandy dunes.
Sliding in while no one notices you ~ waves of silence.
All in Peace.

*

<u>"You Know what I meant?"</u>
Landing in a Spaceship, animals feeling Mind Object.
Left us numerous Pyramids to show us who they were.
Dissociating the Ego; The Question Is the Answer!
Hiding & surviving; It's a massive jungle;
It's every day life for some ~ up at dawn.
The Real Response is beyond words.
When you ask of Yourself ~
Who Am I? Just sit and say
I AM NATURAL SILENCE
And there won't be an answer.
The answer is in the stillness.

Solomente Uno

I'll skip the flying & swimming with sharks. She makes the Pan.
There's 7.5 billion + Individual Minds attached to the Planet!
"I can't even get my 1st chakra going!" ~ He's Joking.
Labial Love bursting out of a beating heart vortex!
Then there's Birds & the Bees making tantric puja!
There's Adam & Eve's magical enchantment!
Looking for the Love ~ we are the Love!
In each one of us

*

Viva Goa for Conscientious Objectors

'The ego is meant to be there because without the ego,
there would be no such thing as transcendence of ego.
Maya is necessary and needed for there to be a Buddha'
Exploring seeing what works ~ Reactions in your data Programming.
Ability to accept what is...Trying different options in the playground.
Creating Reality, being created, creativity, Response to inner space.
Purity when there is no You ~ Poets cannot fail winning the Smile.
Trying to Represent the Truth! Not taking sides.
"I don't want any Control over anybody!"
"The Prime Minister doesn't dance or his cabinet!"
"When she was conceived it was fully out of love!"
"Yes the kids need to know their dads; I'm sorry!"
Make vows before having children for the clarity!
"I can't stand it anymore, what's the point?"
"There is no point, we've gone past the point of no return"
You never found what you were looking for; "Bye Bye."
A Numbers game ~ Infinity means you never stop.

17

Saying to Yourself

What makes you happy? Very Sweet Love ~ full Open heart.
There'd be something wrong with me if I didn't love it!
Keep looking up at the lights on the way to Heaven.
Got to check yourself ~ having a word with myself!
Tonight she could tell me it's over forever ~ again!
It could have been so amazingly cool.
Each person on the Planet is Loved.
Let your heart sing.

*

In All you see ~ Proactive Oneness

Intuition * Unity * Co*creating ~ loving one another.
Logical birth mind ~ this Consciousness of Control
and its roots are Fear! Angels, Goddesses Activated.
Mind Illumination from gentleness of heart chakra.
All of us are burning in Eternal Love * Light.

*

Channeling ~ Rhythm Self

"It's a beautiful World and it's our home"
It's supposed to happen, you have to accept everything ~
that happens because it's all connected from the Totality.
It's all meant to be, what do you have to say about it?
Don't Think be Still, whatever comes out ~
won't be from your Hanky Panky thoughts.
Selfish gene, we have Choice all the Time
going along with conditioned reactions?
Ignorance, suffering or pain is optional ~
Instead of feeling Anger feel Compassion.
Again you know what I mean? Nothing.

<u>*They know what I mean!*</u>
"I give up ~ I surrender I'm going to the Banyan tree"
Independence day, don't wanna cause a riotous effect!
'Our goal just trying to keep sane through each day'
It's when you don't have any choice you're a Slave!
"Do not worry until the Doctor arrives"
GMO. coconut trees blowing in a tropical ocean breeze.
Not realising they're Alive ~ told to live in the sin model.
Challenging the 'I'm Right, you're Wrong perspective'
Total equality because of who we all are ~
not the Identification of an Isolated Matrix Illusion.
The future is only in your Imagination ~ be here now.
Love enslaved by a confused Voodoo priestess ~
"It's a broken relationship!" She peeled off Taboos.
In the groove melting each other's expectations.
You can only do it from the Present ~ SPACE
Who's in the delusion of wanting too much?
"It seems real but its platitudes, full bullshit!"
Everything is omnipresent ~ Consciousness

*

<u>*DNA ~ Flow*</u>
The blessed blood cells carrying everything you know ~
How are you ~ You can still be yourself wherever you are.
Can be FUN ~ What else do we do?
Distracted from doing it at the Bed & Breakfast Moksha Motel.
Enjoying the journey ~ preconception, anticipation, delectation ~
Enjoying every moment of delight, 'coitus a tergo' consommation!
How nice to put our whole attention on what we're doing.
Fully Feeling the Experience.

Nisargadatta's Tao Garden
Time is Precious ~ that's for sure!
'Dhyan' ~ 'Meditation' can't translate it!
Emptiness clears the mind. Cleansing ~ Inside the tears.
You can control it without controlling it ~
Face it ~ Look at him in the eyes as a person.
The inner ~ outer oceans coming together.
'We are the Love'
*

Watch your breath
In the Space ~ between the Stars.
He had a total rebuild, now happy.
We have the Program of darkness.
An absence of light, try 'Vipassana'
Insight feeling the Connecting ~
'This Supreme flower is you'
*

'You are free to drink' ~ Concept
Meditation knows the dangers of all manifested programs
of the mind. Just watching the Projections*Breathe in Love
exhale Love ~ Mind can't tolerate the light of Awareness.
"There is no Religion ~ there is only human beings
who share their experiences with spontaneous Love"
Everybody is an Angel ~ be your*self. "I've come
to rehabilitate myself from the Insanity of the World"
You are your own Satguru. Given the keys; What's this?
"Are you ready for Love?" ~ "Where is Love?"
It triggers something going beyond the mind.
'High in his Space Program'

Whatever the Desire

"Baba there's no house in India without potatoes…."
The sisters of Venus ~ we make our own Pagan heaven.
There is a devil invented by the Church, he doesn't exist!
That Greed exists in us; Blaming it on an Imaginary figure.
He invented the apple ~ cast out for having a glorious fuck,
when he gave man a dick and an erection to propagate fate!
Tantra is the Truth ~ enjoying ecstasy, freely feeling naturally
not an Imaginary paradise, its perfect beauty in her green eyes.
And these demons are robbing the joy out of your life ~ Again!
Makes you go in guilt and suffering, full of bad things their sin.
PsyOps; They'll kill Love put you into another dense frequency.
Call it a F… Holy War but it's Hatred, draining all y/our energy!
Dominion over the World, for what? Money, Power, Insecurity.
Waking up people from heavens and hells of Religious Authority!
Experience being in the moment ~ the senses of life's existence.
You won't get birth again ~ Climaxing in the Cosmic!

*

Proper rinsing it.

GOA ~ "I've come here NOT to be miserable loving you!"
You wanna stay connected send a Cosmic Spirit Postcard.
Why would they stop me walking up the hill and taking off?
Friends are the ones who'd let you crash ~ on their sofa!
Yoginis' Tantric King ~ erotically, surreal, love poesia in flow.
'24hour, no shower, full power' ~ energy on the dance floor!
Institutionalised at Curlies ~ beside an Indian Dora Maar.
Truth of being ~ It's fabulous to have a sultry muse, darling.
'Everything In Existence Is Divine'
'Space Travel Is Time Travel'

<u>Broke their word of Honour!</u>
Beauties beyond the human imagination ~
Garuda the biggest Eagle ~ Vishnu's powerful Spaceship.
Fire dynasty throughout the Universe with blessings of Indra.
Soma and crystal mixed by Apsaras, Celestial women on Earth.
At death they're waiting to escort you to their Planet.
Why close the door on those delights?
They won't let you in Heaven after that!

*

<u>What's the Time Baba?</u>
Contemplating AIDS poisoning ~ conceptual Witch hunting!
"I'm not broken, it's not a problem" Then find a new sickness!
Back to Cosmic Space walks, stepping out of Mind; Stillness.
Acceptance of the Mystery of Life ~ that is Enlightenment.
'Catch my smile'

*

<u>Sit still Now.</u>
Total Response not Reaction….FREE TO ~
I am a body and I'd like to make Love with that nymph!
Keep it Legal! "If it makes your heart sing"
'Life has no meaning it's always becoming ~'
There is no one ~ 'Consciousness in Awareness'
Timeless ~ being here in an Instant of Infinity.
'Thought is Time' ~ In Quantum Consciousness.
Your Memories telling You >'I AM ^NOT THAT '<
I don't have a beginning or an end or any duality ~
The Divine is within me not outside ~ I AM ALREADY.
Transcending the roots of Form You're just being Yourself.
'From life to life ~ playing the game of existence to the end'
"Things is the way they's is"

But not on me.

"Senility is wasted on most people" ~ no alternative reality feeling!
CLARITY of AWARENESS, the Master remaining as clear as a bell.
People afraid of what is True! Are you a willing Slave or a Siddha?
The Mayans didn't go anywhere they're still in their etheric Temples
vibrating at a higher invisible rate ~ renounce God become yourself.
Your Realisation there's no Time ~ Surrender is not about choices...
Enlightenment being in the now ~ in the immortal Presence of Truth.
"No sense hanging on to anything, we're just clay" resonating pots.
You're a light to your own feelings ~ "I don't do Muppets!"
"The end of pleasure is Painful the end of Pain is pleasurable"
'Life is full of Experiences' ~ Marriage is to Live in the moment!
Enjoying the beauty ~ enjoying the mystery.

*

Sniff it, Snort it, Bosch it!

Pink champagne, Cocaine breakfast, Puri bhaji, Masala chai!
No Intellectuals or nanobotanic fruit & veggies in the Zen studio.
Running right into Death's GMO arms ~ Dumping it in the Ocean!
You enjoy the Space ~ Onboard you pay the price and more.
'At Dasaswamedh Ghat Brahma sacrificed ten horses to pave
the path for the return of Shiva after his period of banishment'
Can you feel Heaven's Inspiration ~ transcendently, letting it come?
River of Samsara, holy Goddess Ganga ~ washing your karma away!
Fearless exploration helps soft machine genes swim beyond dualities.
'Smiling faces in front of Virupaksha Temple, Hampi' ~ Bom Shankar!
"I like dropping into other Worlds!" And you Jiddu Krishnamurti?
'Meditation is Freedom from thought*movement in ecstasy of truth'
You are the Foundation of the Hearth ~ no other.

Software Programs
Who is practicing the Military Form of Ashtanga Yoga?
Now the Philippines is closed, no more cheap fleeces!
The fatalistic Political failure to change the World ~
Not more sense but more destructive capability!
"Oceans of information ~ not a drop of wisdom"
Maybe everything's already fucked, grass for Trauma!
Opening up Colorado Star gates to the Cosmic whole
*

Demo * Crazy
"Vote for me and I'll decide what parties you can have,
celebrating being out at night!" ~ What freedom is that?
"I want to do what I want, when I want, where I want
with whom I want ~ not causing harm to anyone else."
Such a heart breaking moment when I had to leave my Lover.
Not in the here & now ~ I'm not here to feel guilty, how stupid!
Giving her positive feedback seeing the divine in your partner.
"Give me some good Illusions, I'm not going to say No"
'Having a female touch without a female in the house'
Let Love flow to letting go wanting ~ to be free to be.
*

Dream Island
"Coke it's an ego drug,
nothing for the heart ~"
The future/brain/chemistry is unimaginable.
Shiva Valley it's sharing in Nataraj vibration!
*Its Energy is everything*let them all go there.*
Fantastic vibes ~ "We're each other's wisdom"

Him & 2 tubes

An afternoon with your 'Crack' ~ this land is so unstable!
"The last one went 'Bang' and I've never had one since"
Raw nature Alchemist ~ he puts his magic into it.
"It's good to have a hot Russian on your side"
Having the guns choosing who lives & dies!
"Life showed me its angelic wings"

*

Rentanotherhappyslave.com

"I liked it before they had any fences...."
Kept like dogs loyal to their Royal Master.
Thank Fuck we don't live in that Mind-set!
"the more dust the more they were havin' it"
"I don't worry about the Planet now ~
reassuring that nature will return eventually"
Comin' & goin' ~ as you please Cosmically.
"No one here's gotta go to work on Monday"
Drop out, 'Experiencing what you are believing'
Beside emerald green waters ~ dazzling white sand,
bluest sapphire sky, sparkling diamonds, infinite stars.
An international airport on the horizon ~ An unreal mirage
of a concrete, plastic, GMO, plutonium, irradiated paradise!
Tranceman Khan, he is a true Sufi ~ spinning like a Cesium top!
Paul Delvaux's tram shed under a full moon with opalescent nudes.
Taught *light being* meditation from Dolphins somewhere in a future.
Bringing back divine magic absolutely ~ Languid, sweet and smooth.
Any kind of honey "It's food for the Queen!" ~ Super waxy
It is good on your tongue!

'We Kiss'

We caress gently ~ intimately with Love not a FGM. rusty file!
Ask her sublime drama Guru for a taste of organic Prasad.
'3 times a week for stronger, visibly longer hair' ...Really?
Free to flow or to follow the rules, laws on whose Authority?
Free to do what you're told, free to simply go out yur mind!
Freedom is not a Supra real state of a Mind. * Wei Wu Wei.
'Freedom is a Supra*real state of an opened up mind Space'
'Truth is what shows us we're already free, here now ~ '
"One political prisoner of Conscience is one too many"
Dancing anytime ~ for the moon, for the lotus, for the bliss,
divine devotion with passion, with an open heart and smile!
They'll be partying the night away by switching on their light.
Sweet heart Kaleidoscopes & she's getting all Tantra'd up!

*

Drudge Life

"That's the Worst, that KILLS the SPIRIT, for Sure!"
Unfriended, Free & single ~ If I want to do it I'll do it!
It's called 'Crack' in a tube & You got the Biggest Dose!
Activating the proper Programs having a lot of connectivity.
"You get down on the floor and interact with your children."
Just go with it, be here now, Life is life, death is alive too!
'If it's meant to be it will be' ~ Diving In Power * in Leela.
Not in a Black slave market, sold & bought for money!
Eggs & bacon; Rape & pillage, deviant & corrupt!
Final statement ~ 'Karma's a groovy thing'
Love everybody ~ creating an atmosphere.
"We snort coke, we drink cocktails, boring!"
"There's a Monster in the cot!" Try Psytrance for dummies.
The Rave party is happening ~ Going into transcendental!
"As long as you are smiling inside enjoy the MDMA trip."

Back in the day

"They had hours & hours of blanket bombing!
Obliterated their Cathedral and anyone about.
When Bombs hit next door ~ infernos were raging.
Fighting the flames, hopeless in ruins, the people!"
"Desperately, insane searching for our loved ones!"
Now we'll have to forge a new national Identity Mabel!
Where is the rage, the melodrama; Where is everyone?
"Lost me auntie, uncle and three cousins, I'll never forget"
Defiant in adversity; "We'll fight them on Brighton's beaches,
we'll fight them in the streets, in the hills, on the Palace balcony"
We will never surrender to Tyranny ~ Shot all their Royal family!

*

ENOS' Procreation

The first motivated, trained chimp to go around Planet Earth ~
Flew into space aboard Mercury Atlas 5 on November 29, 1961.
"If you don't put passion into it you won't break a string"
I really like to suck that passion ~ fruit! Beautifully natural.
Thinking coded gene ~ only Intention to survive is its Reality.
Self-sacrifice, puzzle of Altruism, prime behaviour ~ Why is it?
Objective study of ants, observing patterns of the human species.
Read about that 'Manhattan Project' as a Spiritual undertaking?
Taking walks through enchanted, sacred forests.

*

Random Apocalypse?

Rwanda segregation aided a genocidal mind-set, massacred Tutsis!
He took all his feelings and harvested a field of organic vegetables ~
How to get a Surreal perspective, what's the elements of revelation?
"Drudge again that's the worst, killing your soul, for sure, don't do it!"
Doom, destruction ~ Saving the Planet through creativity and Spirit.
Felt it was a dichotomy, duality, paradox, ultimately it's a Divine Gift.

*Pure Juicy Satori * Is just as Real*
ABSENSE ~ ESSENSE, RADIANCE.
The flowering of Love Consciousness
Choosing to be in a state of Responsefulness ~
In meditation, not a holy entertaining distraction.
Figuring out how to be inside a Pin Ball machine.
Tilt, tilt, tilt be a good person or be a mad f... cunt!
Sitting on the beach drinking fresh Coconut juice.
"You can hate me, that's OK; I'm not here really"
Less of a Reaction to L O VE ~ Knowing the Tree.
Giving All Heart Baba.
*

Humility Avatar ~ REFLECTIONS
"Self development is all Arrogance;
As if nature made a mistake!"
'The World Is Perfect'
The reference to Maya,
*Yourself * In this body.*
'It's All Intuitive'
*

One drop at a time ~
"I live by Intuition ~ I am truly its servant."
How do I know this is ME? "I can't seem to live without it"
All the trouble in the World ~ from this 'ME' ~ BEING.
Police preserving law and order in central Holy City!
Spontaneous 'Cinema Verite' ~ what am I looking for?
The Form of our own full filament ~ blue Sapphire eyes.
You are Not the Doer ~ calling on healthy balance.
Seeing the 'blockages' ~ Witnessing of Clarity ~
Finding your innermost door by going deeper.
Into the most sublime bliss of silent, stillness.

'Bodge, Scarper & Sons'

Neem fertiliser only for Export ~ Organic India burnt to ashes!
Burkas on the beach, alcohol poisoning, negative violence.
You stay in the Present ~ it all works out fine
or you bring it into the mind! www.Illogical.om.
Holy cows are supposed to eat grass not Sheep's brains!

*

Listen, what the fuck is that!

My heart jumped at the thought of making love with you ~
Expressing the Sunshine ~ enjoying existence of Presence.
Putting that Shiva sticker on it! Anything with a heart.
Goa Convoy ~ A citizen of Planet Earth.
"If I find you lovely, do I love you?"
COSMICALLY ALL BLISSED UP.
Can you ultimately let her go in loving light?
I forgive her and fly on ~
Can feel absolutely if it's real.
Sparkling eyes, fully smiling face.
Ecstasy oozing positives ~ Bliss up!
Now I've become an old memory of..
Loving completely Open and free.

*

Not Happening with 9 Bar ~ Trance Party

"There's not enough of the switched on people to make the energy!"
No one's allowed to wear a Bikini, Salutation. These are the Rules!
Sisters' honour, told a lie, dying avoiding slavery in the Royal harem.
Sati, simple-minded sacrifice but the Caliph never got to touch them.
What's it all about? Is it about getting to the top of the food chain
and listening to holy cows cry ~ choking on another plastic bag?
"I am so unhappy son ~ what would your father say about this?"
'Feudalistic time is still existing here Now'

Orange DDT Opera

Dude open your eyes ~ Tao master's still smiling.
All people are good ~ part of the Sun and Moon.
Walking barefoot ~ feeding the Earth with Stardust.
"Just give it up ~ You never having an opinion!"
Don't touch anything, especially Codex, just get on with it.
Living in a natural state of total Response with yourself ~
Watching your own Karma ~ Expressions of Meditation.
The 'Me' wants the revenge but not the 'I'
There is No You ~ Look at that f…. Muppet!

*

Slap & Stun!

"S/he had it comin' now get over it
or I'll give you another one!"
If you're awake get real;
Yeah you know it hurts!
Mixing of all the 'Gunas'
The root of Fear & Love.

*

A legendary Enfield trip!

Party Animals, Hot senses ~ "Thou shalt not….?"
All are Happy ~ Very good advice for your natural
Super Sensitive Aura sleeping freely on the beach.
'Protect us from illusions' Pinball Wizard, 'Tickety Boo'
'Come to Varanasi to leave your body behind, transmute'
Every atom, molecule, neutrino, particle is Alchemy.
Bhakti Devotion ~ attaching you to pure conscience.
Thinking we're separate ~ We're part of the water!
'And now for something completely different'
We have to be kind to one another ~
Eventually finding balance for us all.

Seagulls & Garudas dancing in the rain
Fully Identifying with performing our Function ~
Inside is emptiness and we're fillin' it up with shit!
I have to stay Present ~ It's a Gift ~ being it, crystal bright.
6 million light years across the Galaxy! A Big Conception!
They're getting older but living longer ~ all is Vibration.
Amazing energies being realised in this natural World.
*'No Self ~ No problem' * Just infinite ~ Space frequency.*
Living the Love Feeling

*

Married to Poison

Can't always land weaponised Drones in a remote village square
or right into a Hacker's bedroom; They don't have a f.... chance!
Only humans can think about God and murdering ~ not animals.
Travelling through 84,000 species ~ I wanna hold onto the light!
Sadhus have no luggage, no attachments, no pain while they exit.
A person with nothing to lose is glad, not a materialist slave to toys.
Where are all the Spiritualists hiding? Maya is all false, it's not there!
Most vegetarians don't wanna be in the slaughtering, dead animal trade.
We're still accepting & respecting super hallucinations, mirages on call.
You can't expect mystical things happening in front of a commercial
crowd ~ different dimension; No emotions, no intuition, desensitised,
brainwashed, insane, exploding Atomic, Napalm bombs for salvation!
IDF. at the Temple mount; they shot his small son then they shot him!
Maya's function to keep you trapped, into these channels of delusions.
There's only you with a Baba and a chillum, teleporting in Mustang.
Divine energy playing with your illusional energy ~ 'My, me, mine & I'
Never sleeps, awake in your own dream, travels thru multi dimensions
not many know about! Demi-God enhanced life not a final destination.
'Swaraj' why wait ~ for Eternity with Krishna living beyond Heaven.
Me and my pulsating Heart transplanted Chakra.

TOGETHERNESS
Totally in the groove with you ~
My groove grooving deeply in your soft groove ~
Building your shelter next to Iceland! "We're dead
it doesn't really matter" ~ change our World Asap app!
People hit their limits, BSE. nailed that holy, mad cow!
Indian man with a Big Bullock standing on his bollocks!
Seeing it getting so bad can't hide or pretend a dystopia.
1000 Nuclear waste tankers alight on the blazing horizon.
No more fish in the Pacific Ocean ~ Clickety, Clicking gills!
Radiation poisoning, the whole biosphere's sick with GMOs!
Perpetual motion, cold fusion, plasma energy, solar powers.
A clear blue sky, patterns of Chemtrails; for Your Own Safety!
Growing meat from stem cells in India, cloning more pigs in China!
Police overtaking on a blind bend ~ let me get the fuck outta here!
Like a rat up a drain pipe; You can fuck it & eat it if that's all you know!
No chance of having a real woman ~ Miss World on four legs!

*

Super duper Stupa.
1st Primal, 2nd sex procreation, 3rd personal power in the world,
4th Love in the heart, 5th all communication, 6th is Intellect ~
7th realisation ~ Self-actualisation of the Cosmic reflection.
"I've channeled it" Who's the withholder who's the beholder?
"Make it happy ~ the more happiness everywhere the better."
On some level I want to be as before, loving you passionately!
It's about where you put your plant pot ~ Sunrays bursting in.
Miracles for F r e e but you gotta bring me lunch and a smile.
"I'm raising the dead but who gives a Fuck?" Wow, Kapow!
Your body is a F I R E ~ hot, clear sandalwood, no smoke.
There's someone sitting in the middle of the 'Padma Kosha'
Just be conscious of what's happening now!

<u>Busted beside Lake Titicaca!</u>
Switching it off but then you're not left with what you like!
"I don't know anyone who sells Ketamine or Solaris do you?"
Sucky, sucky the first one's free! She'll bring her bag of Ice.
"Every Tuk-Tuk driver can sell you a tola of weed or meow!"
Cocaine Society where everyone's on Marching Powder.
'How to be Liberated from Unconscious actions ~
when 'Ignorance Is Bliss!' 'Don't waste your Time'
Seeing what it does to people! What makes you happy?

*

<u>"I'm the Party you've been looking for!"</u>
"Love is not an art it is Life to us!" ~ Feeling energies.
"When they come they'll come for what you Love"
Changing my Insight ~ A higher force is in us.
Opening for it to blossom in your heart.
"If he's in it he can't be out of it"
We are all one in one.

*

<u>Simple & Natural</u>
Giving the Gift of Healing ourselves ~
A bit of what you like ~ Unconditionally.
Don't ever ask me for anything but Love ~
They only want romance when they want it,
anything else is your own responsibility mate!
Feeding her, fulfilling all her dreams & expectations.
She loves you for what you can give her! Sneak a peek..
They'll make you responsible if they're having a bad time!
Why pretend ~ for those not having to remember the Truth?
Teaching them to be parasites, divorce him & onto the next.
"I'm not here to tell you right from wrong ~ You know it"
You chose to sacrifice someone who truly loved you.'
"The Universe knows best"

Wank Dogmas

Hey man, stuck only in the senses ~ can't Transcend!
Can't deny your feelings ~ Life is Experiencing N O W
Questioning Faith would be philosophy ~ a rhapsody.
Religion is only about belief ~ No Spirit.
Crystal healing is being validated ~
Giving her permission to live her life.
Confidence to witness fear, negative projection!
The World is held together by small kindnesses.
There's no enemies, everybody is a winner ~
And they want to throw stones, losing ground!
Blessing y/our children

*

Mutual Funding * Saving People!

'To speak to someone who has no self respect is dishonoring.'
Not dependent on you, meet strength of character, Dung eater.
Stopping all Barbaric practices ~ cool off, lots of street beds!
Killing each other until they've had enough then they'll talk.
Wolves don't have facial expressions or ever wag their tails.
Yellow eyes ~ basically you're just a piece of meat to them!
"Oh didn't we tell you there's a Tiger missing from the Zoo?"
If it's meant to happen we'd like to offer you...
Psychic healing ~ connecting with your higher self.
Inspiration, have you come to believe in yourself yet?
"Self development leads to Madness ~ how will you ever
Know that you're finished?" ~ More and more, it's never ending!
Unhappy unless they're on somethin' stuck up their root chakra.
Healing ~ You were made ALWAYS PERFECT.
It's a gift to give ~ I can show you Heaven.
Your ego has to die to become like this ~
but that's how you get a feather!

Vermillion Monarch
'I Spiked the Queen!'
"Oh look at all the pretty colours….
Smoking a big reefer on the balcony!
Festival raves on the Summer Palace's lawns.
She looks like a right royal bitch, uncool in fluro.
Didn't know what it was but they could feel it too.

*

Message coming
"I wanna manifest as a big bag of dope and smoke it myself"
Coak from the Valleys… "Everyone can chop a line!"
Lizards it's a metaphor ~ manifestations of D'evil.
"A monkey could make it with a hammer and a nail!"
Grateful dead Acid * full alchemy made under the stars.
We're all connected ~ Life comes for FREE, Being there.
Absorbing, enjoying it, aware of fluttering butterflies.
If you feel it's a Matrix, illusion, duality ~
You become a Baba living in a cave,
reincarnating as an inner Spaceman.
Billions of galaxies in our Universe!
Light a candle * shine the light!
Life is for Living

*

Taken straight to Stardom
Shiva Valley ~ "It's alive the Energy man!"
Energy * Is * Everything, got me out Alive.
We have to protect its essence ~ B O O M * B O O M!
Sleep, death, consciousness at rest ~ being yourself.
Total meditational Response ~ Open channels flowing.
The faeries are telling you something; making decisions.
The Gods are playing with us.

If the Slave is willing...
The most beautiful virgin girls in the King's Empire
queuing up, lying on a table to be openly examined.
Which one has the most beautiful, sweet pussy cat smile,
who is dreaming to be chosen as the Queen of my harem?
Licking bowls of cream in little sips between her lips.
Who has the Goddess' spicy, sensual hips?

*

All In Silence
Burn the last of the Sun out of your body.
Evil is in the wrong approach to problems.
Needs self-enquiry not opinions or reactions
just a response from a contemplative state ~
When you read them they wake up your feelings.
Poetry has to have feeling ~ showing us it's not in the words.
'From out the mouth of Babes ~ leading you to heavenly space'

*

Control of Everything!
The Master will do whatever s/he wants; Who has the POWER?
Hand on a Live wire ~ Everything is Spontaneous ~ Life Cosmic.
"One cannot be killed, no tyranny" "If you stand in your Truth,
nothing can touch you." ~ There are no Ifs in FREE SPACE !
Up for a bit of rock & roll!

*

Attention Villagers
1. Your village was bombed because you harboured
Vietcong in your village
2. Your village was bombed because you gave help
to the Vietcong in your area.
3. Your village was bombed because you gave food to
the Vietcong. USMC Leaflet. Operation Phoenix.

Hallucifarian Scenario

We're still looking ~ Even a star can't fulfill being the Sun.
This wanting to get there when you're already there.
Looking for something ~ It's all bliss in life.
Here ~ present in the Omnipresence.

*

Valium & Electrolytes

'The man who snow boarded down Everest naked'
The Japanese 'lunatic'... we've found conscious!
'Goa with no labels' ~ Don't just fit me in!
Detachment from holographic projections.
You start over with Instant Karma ~
You're lucky you found your joy ~ so Enjoy!
Some objects are really lovely, beautiful visions, co creating ~
I do believe in heaven, if you're experiencing bliss ~ I like that one.

*

Vaikuntha

Spiritual Universe ~ where we come from...
Here is a reflection of what's there ~ 'Moksha'
Time to STOP, no good if you can't breathe ~
They'll let you do the murder then get money from you!
"Is your heart singing ~ we're in this beauty together"
Watching the World get light.

*

Shiva Aromatic

Now our tolerance has made us intolerant ~ intolerable.
"Why should I tolerate you when you won't tolerate us?"
'Sex is communication with someone they love'
Pointing the direction ~ you give them the ball.
He's done shit, lost his innocence, no joyfulness.
"Gods are cunts!" ~ You just do the right thing.

In Love with Lust
"I'm a Pagan man worshipping at the Temple of Pan"
I go where I wanna go when I wanna go.
"My life is a total pursuit of Pleasure"
"You learn that being miserable is a waste of time"
I want the Inspiration, the magic, divine bliss,
with you ~ the Endless Lover's kiss

*

Why are we Expecting?
"I always stepped out of it like that" Starting to rub ~
Listening to the Hard drive, all that redundant stuff!
"OK Baby I'll meet you in the next dimension!"
"Gotta have the Spiritual in there Baba!"
Feeling not Thinking.

*

Smelling Contradictions.
"I want some of that" ~ Written into an Orgasmic haiku.
That's when you become enlightened with no Zen name.
There is no should or shouldn't ~ it is what it is, ain't it?
Here only to become Conscious ~ Not Drones over Mecca!
Unfathomable Pain of Catholicism's Torture chambers et al.
You don't have to be rich to enjoy LSD for new insight.
Transcendence doesn't bother you anymore, not reacting,
A C C E P T A N C E ~ If Your Heart Sings.
Switch the light on to see it's bollocks, no awareness.
Selling you something negative for the pain not healing it.
"You make vast Profits rebuilding countries you destroyed!"
Creative Inshallah Perspective believing in it to be T R U E.
Conditioned to choose the Illusional, delusional, ego mind.
They're still bleating sheep, has to come from within You!
Yes by enslaving our Hearts & Minds ~ 'We Liberated you!'

Cuming Together * In Enchantment

I'll cum whenever, wherever your cake wants me to cum.
To be a sunny mango in tune with your hot Venus Moon
I'd come for your natural, homemade jam custard sponge
if it had your lovely sweet nectar dripping into me.
I'd come for ambrosial fruits of Eros or just a cupcake caress
because I know you'd embrace my rapturous cock au jelly.
I'd come inside your melting oven there I'd be in heaven.
I'd come for the joy of grinding your fresh cafe au lait ~
its taste and smell, percolating, exuding the most sublime.
I'd come if for only a plain croissant or dainty scone and
let my voracious tongue lick your succulent, ruby lips.
I know it'd all be delicious and we'd become delirious
eating Sicilian cheesecake inside your smiling cheeks.
I'd cum for syrupy strawberry and mango French toast
spread with organic, raw jungle honey, sucking your finger tips.
I'd come for sticky clity, toffee pudding, drizzling lust just to see
you smile, unleash your Goddess fountain showering it over me.
I'll cum too for my favourite Ice cream, you're my perfect dream.

*

I'd like to pound forever your exotic wet spice, releasing beautiful
delicacies, their aroma and seductive fragrances transcending into
our superbe paradise. I'd cum for your unimaginable raw chocolate
sorbet or smooth labial mousse and let my phallus delve deep inside
your Angel's moist grotto, whipping cream pleasure. Your exalted
buttocks writhing up in extreme delirium, wildly throbbing, pouring
out like excited magma streams over our sweating, dripping skin.
I'd cross the radiant Universe to suck your sensational hard lemons
squeezing their tangy juices of temptation into my yearning mouth.
I'll indulge feeling the lascivious Black forest between your thighs ~
Penetrate soft velvety layers, nibbling its quivering little red cherry.

In anticipation of such salacious delices I'd open a magnum of
Bubbly for the joy of loving such a gorgeous arse to die for, tight
as a hazelnut, so divine. Knowing for that time your offering of
intense passion would all be mine. I'd give you my erotic, Tantric
lollypop to suck and suck and suck and never want your mouth
to stop in a lustfully, felatio Cosmic fuck. I'd kneel before you,
a orgiastic cornucopia, overflowing with desires. We'd consume
each other's hearts and souls all through the night, cooking in
your carnal, blazing fires, melting us together into Creme delight.
I'd cum just to feel the entrancing touch of your gentle hand in
mine, looking up to the stars in your sparkling eyes twinkling
down on me. Giving to each other timeless liberation, sexually,
multi*orgasmic flames beside midnight's languid ocean ~ holding
you in pure ecstasy, entwined in the sand. I'd love to share slices
of your sensual gateau filled with infinite blisses. I'd devour you
fill your light being with the infinity of extra-sensory kisses.
Our spirits cuming together for this surreal, magical feast ~
Allowing love's Tantric flow to live in us forever being free

*

And Loved
Remember that we're all blessed ~ You're in the light shining bright.
We're Loved and Loved and Loved and Loved and Loved and Loved
and Loved and Loved and Loved and Loved and Loved and Loved ~
it's the only thing keeping the smoley together dispelling the darkness.
Going undercover into the heart. "Tell me the magic ~
what is the spell?" All the pulling power you can muster!
Hey OK we're all full of light and that's very jolly;
what about those lost in the Fear?
It's as simple as that,
You are the Love ~
Just be the Love.

Baba Day Vibrations
Psychedelic Saris, Muslim Feng Shui, Cosmic reflections ~
When tripping don't look in Narcissisms' mirror but tell yourself
how much you love yourself, what a beautiful Heart you are!
"I Love Earth and I love the wild bushes along Venus' shore"

*

Real Freedom Gene
I have come for a glorious memory ~ but it's gone!
Changing each moment ~ being together in bliss.
"Come on me, come again" 'Manage your Craving'
The smile in your eyes tells me everything about
the light inside ~ All part of this Cosmic truth.

*

Nose on a dog.
Freaky hippie chic ~ 'No woman no cry'
"It's good for us to cry ~ taught him how to box!"
"I've seen a lot of amazing things at the Omni Theatre!"
Don't have the love, instead addicted to the dramatic.
Inflict as much damage as possible making the most profit!
WHO ME? Now you've fallen for something that isn't real.
Notions in you leading you to higher dimensional designs.
"Skunk revolutionised the Smoking World, troppo THC"
The Idea came from Space & DNA and in the apples.
"You are making it Exist" ~ they're on the same stage.
'The Man who fell in Love with the Moon lunatic'
"YES" Trippy, hippie magic ~ It's all poetry.
You got to be able to hit the delete button!
It's the same river running through you.
The nature of the 'me' part to do it;
There's the 'I' part too ~
"I never say mine"

*'Oui Oui' * Personality.*
*'On vie les reves' * It's up to you!*
Changing our brainwaves ~ "Why be like that?"
"Be nice"
*

<u>*You Feel ~ the Vibes*</u>
When you're dead it's all gone ~
Slowly dying each & every moment…
Guilt eating away at you until you come clean.
"I'm not a customer to them I'm an enemy!"
Don't give me that I wanna live in the bliss.
They picked the wrong bus ~ the eyes on you!
*

<u>*Angels are good*</u>
Psychopaths they have no human feelings or empathy ~
They Keep on Terrorising Us; Malleable for Machiavelli!
The Sun can never know darkness because it's always light.
Absence doesn't make the heart grow fonder ~ be here now.
No need wanting in Real life ~ they think the wanting is Love!
Love doesn't have an absence; Hate is an absence of Love?
It's just duality, opposites, dialectics, polarities, wanting both ~
When you're in emotional depression, Rejection, chain Reaction,
it's hard to find something else, any reflections to be joyful about.
*The Moon is the Moon * The Sun is the Sun.*
*

<u>*Empty Sarcophagus*</u>
"If the sea continues to rise some people will develop gills"
The fear of death ~ love of Life making the chemicals react.
"If you took the sand out of Egypt you'd get an Idea of
what's transpiring" ~ There's powerful Magic going on.
"We even took the Mummies!"

We've stepped in the DNA

*Bottom line ~ Life Continues (Dynamic sperm * fittest gene)*
Love is not defining all the differences ~ age, colour, cute I Q.
It's a gift falling in your voluptuous kisses, being in love with you.
In your heart of hearts love is tingling feelings on your wet lips ~
Ending our Love affair how did we take a dream so seriously?
They have the same functions, different program, lost their trust.
"It's not caste pretending but they just won't accept outsiders"
'Love and let live' ~ It's that simple

*

King of the Bus Pass.

They knew the f.... rules, the routine ~ End of the line!
They have to learn, you have to teach them, Social Spirit.
Design to take away their strength, take away the discipline
of a rowdy bunch of stupid idiots. Who's the Boss around here?
Who can predict what's coming? ~ They can control
YOU if they break the Human Mentally and physically!
Descended from slaves, "What shall I retrieve Master?"

*

"I had to hate him to leave him"

You can lead your favourite pony to water but you can't ~
make her drink or become a lascivious hedonist, only for you.
Defensive Mind-set ~ Really hurts when you're dumped, rejected!
Full acceptance, knowing the mysteries of life ~ diversity of nature.
It's goin, goin, goin, gone I had to go with its immediate momentum,
otherwise I'd have tumbled down ~ just stopped by the water's edge!
Wheels on wheels, flower of life ~ let the engines keep on running.
Conditioned to believe, "If it doesn't upset the Buddha you can do it"
'Get rid of all the elements that don't work' ~ Inconsequentiality.
You can talk the talk ~ Now can you walk the walk?
Free Pleasure Forever

Pilot Baba

Eco activists, not plague, horror, monsters, terrorist aliens!
"I think I need a Jellybean from an Off-Planet Android"
I like swimming with Russian mermaids on a Cliticat.
She married him and became one of his 366 wives!
All your Earth dreams are over ~ I can't believe it.
"Thank God she wasn't a Bikini Atoll bunny!"
Shocking! You gotta put it out there!
"Drop the World" ~ "Let it go"

*

Just Another Vibration

They're still here ~ Invisible spectrums.
A handsome skull ~ flaming next to you!
"All enlightened people have a sense of ego
I * AM * God, no greater image of oneself"
"I Am Brahma" ~ I Am, still in the mind!
Pop In, "The 'I' calling your name"
Crossing through seven dimensions ~
You don't want to believe that you're dead, that
you don't exist ~ For anyone else except yourself.
Enlightenment ~ there is no 'I'
All those wet dreams are over.

*

A Wizard in the World

"Someone (Lizard) has to run all these sheeple!"
Masons working with the clay for their own glory.
They came to take that role, reacting to the Power!
Humans always talking about 'Me' & 'Mine not Divine'
Life doesn't make any mistakes ~ Holistic Spirit is within all of us.
I live in a Perfect frequency World.
The Sun shines everyday in Goa.

<u>There are no strangers in Love</u>
"Love is not selective * desire is selective"
It'll drop your vibration ~ Rise above animal nature.
Holy shit on the wind ~ in lust feeling a Tulsi vibe
beside the burning Ghats ~ Moksha is always kind.
Cunctipotent Kundalini healing is in your nature to be it.
Creative, if you have it use it ~ life teaches you.
Let the Ashram happen if it happens by itself ~ Spontaneously.
*

Spiritual Demolition
Energetic healers are destroyers ~ Karma light mechanics.
The snake's telling you ~ have no opinions, no projections,
no memory, no past there's only ever now. My hair's on fire!
Self delusional, self mutilation, self hatred, unsolved crimes.
Responding to animals' old patterns, subconscious coming out.
"The Cobras would jump out and come sit with me"
Going through this Transformation willingly ~
Today we solved all the problems of the World.
Because there are none ~ Shiva Mantra chant.
"of course I'm a recluse, what do you think?"
"Kiss my ass, yu ain't from these parts are yu?"
Suspicious, "I might have to shoot you and your family you know?"
Putting me in the swamp; They got a different accent down there.
Shut up!
*

PASSIONATELY
"I feel it's everybody's responsibility to look after the children
Regardless of whose children they are."
Are they with the person who Loves them ~ on the Inside?
They know they're Loved ~ without that they can't Love!
Everyone's a child of the Universe.

45

Paradisiacal Now
'Know yourself like the rest of us ~
Turn within, stop the greed, the selfish opinions'
Ego let it go ~ "Have nothing, want nothing, be
Nothing ~ That will bring you joy; I'm just here.
Smokin' pot taking off the edge of havin'
to leave behind what I adored so much!
All about Love, Kindness and calmness.
Part of my becoming Intuitive ~ Your heart's not open.
Here have a spear, a spare Trident, burning deeply, feel it!
"I don't know what I feel about anything." I love, I can't Love.
How long lost in the same menagerie lookin' for each other?

*

Moksha #11
You know her as much as you know your own heart.
Looking lovingly into your clear smiling hazel eyes.
Feeling all of your divine attributes on my hot skin.
You like your elements, you never have to beg.
Gotta play with it like a pebble in your shoe.
There's no good reasonable reason to have an Opinion!
Children of the Universe communicating through music ~
"The Zen state of No Judgment called Response ~ Meditative"

*

All Lamps Burning are Equal potential!
What is this fire inside her burning bush?
"We're rich but have no money syndrome"
Living within a holistic, sacred lily pond ~
Keeping it clear and pure not Hazmat, toxic dumping!
The body is the lamp ~ 'Me' is the coloured glass.
"We're all angels falling thru Chaos!" 'I' is the light inside.
"I go full Krishna"

<u>No Nightmares here!</u>
Free Spirit ~ through the purity ~ of music.
"You can only come out of Russia cute!"
Only the beautiful are allowed to leave.
Don't take it too seriously; Simple is uncomplicated.
Good to keep those blissful memories, hard to let you go
but that was your decision as I was still fully addicted.
Gotta move with the times ~ have more Ecstasy.
Makes you pretty open to what could happen!
"I like lots of stuff that makes me laugh."
*

<u>Illusional * Maya</u>
"If you drop off the ceiling and land on your head,
it's gonna hurt! Now is now and that's Real,
doesn't matter how much you say it's not!"
Getting it done in your mind is getting it done in your mind!
It's always a good result if you get away with it.
Open face Plan ~ Biometrics, you're essentially Free.
*"You're always free anyway" * Free is going beyond mind.*
*

<u>Kindness</u>
*My heart is Open * feeling, adoring You.*
'528 kHz frequency ~ the tone of Love'
Soft pink sunbeams, elements of calmness.
Got into some concept of existence ~
of why we're alive ~ "I Love You"
*

<u>Rehab Synchronicity</u>
Wherever we go ~ the right transformation.
Scalding water is a lesson to my burning leg.
You go to sleep or does sleep come to you?
Wiping our memories.

Flea Pit Road

Conscious awareness of the Mind ~ Feelings in the body.
The thinking has to STOP when conscious of the Feeling.
If your Attention is not on the Mind, it can feel the body.
We think we are ~ Every moment is an Opportunity
to feel that Cosmic Consciousness flowing Inside.
I've been thinking ~ calmly have a look inside yourself.
Feel what you are beyond the Form ~ in tune with our nature.
Doomed only knowing the Forms, everything will turn to dust.

*

Vanunu & the Kamikaze

Work thru it somehow; Fresh wounds of a concentration camp.
Seeing how far they can go to break your human will.
Let's hope I'm heroic to the end, like some before me.
A smile on your face, in your heart as the nails go in!
Where's 'Skull Splitter' the axe, 'Odin' the brain eater?
This is my sword do you like it? It's called 'Heart Taker'.
We're men we like wars! Me I'd rather enjoy the Harem.
Nout to do with us 'mourire pour les Idée's'- I'll go to Macau!
There's no dignity surviving in a solitary prison cell for years!
At least the monk has the choice to stay or not.
Now who is immune from Radiation poisoning?
Fukushima deep in the currents of a Toxic Ocean.
Radioactive particles * spinning all over this Planet!
And who told the World about the threat of Dimona?
Who was then sacrificed to the fascist oligarchs?
Aluminium in every Nano cell we are breathing.
They're changing our 'Dualism' our reactions ~
Manipulating another accident in our Paradise!
Wo/Man receiving the Sun's blessings on Earth.
All part of this Cosmic Truth.

Voluptuous Nature
Virtual erotica ~ from the heart is more amazingly beautiful!
"I set off all the Alarms wherever I go"
What is in the woman's breast?
Ten in a room and sari's up.
"If you wore a bikini you wouldn't sit with the nudists."
"Rip it all off!" Entering the stream of Love ~ together.

*

Enjoying the Pain
'Who the fuck does he think he is stopping someone protesting?
"You're free to follow ~ You're free to flow"
You in the Universe ~ It's a photon*nano*bio*chronograph
Spinning wheels ~ on fire; Be yourself and get on with it.
"We're not sheep, I'm a Lion but I like sheep!"

*

W H Y?
I Want the b/rain to Stop ~
I want this f.... pain to Stop.
I want Karma's World to Stop.
Bless us with Tantric Bhakti miracles.
Going through all the barriers of aversion.
Face all YOUR Fears, dark magic reflections.
Inside you ~ You know yourself without Ideas.
"I am all things and in all things"
You're not any of these things ~
Just like I'm not the reflection in this mirror!

*

Empirical Greed
Land of debt, home of Mentally ill.
Psycho Babble >:< that's my head!
The Mind is your servant ~ Master.
Some nights he can't close his eyes!

Glowing Bauls

Radiating Joy ~ When you see their Aura
Smiling ~ You gotta SMILE too from Inside!
"Himalayan Rishis not the Rubber mat, AC. Yogis"
Shanti, manifesting charas whenever ~ in their so Big chillums!
Transcending living in the senses of imaginary dreams & desires.
Risking your life, thoughts have no substance, floating in thin air.
Like scratching an itch; Sadhus have higher spiritual aspirations!

*

Solaris Sultan

Which toxic Reich are we in now? Storm troopers at the window.
US Gestapo banging down your front door, waterboarding FEMA.
What really happens; Rambo image or Manning's & Snowden etc?
Slaughtering people, innocent civilians from Apache Helicopters!
Children being murdered with the excuses of Collateral damage!
Not warriors dying in battle with a code of conduct but demons!
Primitive wanting to own the World ~ Really it belongs to nobody.
They contaminated the water to raise prices for Corporate devils!
Live by a riverbank, clean air, solar panels, seeds & happy weeds!

*

Living As Nature.

"The Sound of the Universe ~ We have to tune to that"
She will give you everything you need ~ Merci.
Sitting cross-legged listening to a diggeridoo.
Resonating with brighter Gongs, being healed.
All coming in waves ~ the Perfect frequency.
When you're in Love everyone smiles at you.
You are happy when you're in Love, it's true!
Birds are singing ~ butterflies gently flitting.
We all want that 'In Love' feeling.
Loving everything around you ~ vibrates.

Sugar's Sweetness
Knowing that I Am * Itself in Form ~ in Cosmic Space
Moving in a sea of Consciousness ~ essence
but we think we're separate ~ that we're God!
Understanding the mechanism and allowing it.
"His wife was devout but he never went"
You can't argue with frequency ~ it is as it is.
Sanctifying the whole thing ~ that's L O VE.

*

Not Tuning in to Sing
"There is no black in the Union Jack;" Racist anthems!
"Mud thrown is ground lost" "Blindness is Silence?"
"If you want to find gold you have to dig in the Earth"
Man looking up at the stars at night in an empty desert.
Connected to the Heart ~ it's happening anyway.
'What, where, who, why, how?' 'Go Into free Space'
It's all free ~ Happy, inspired, full of Love & Light.

*

Calling It In
'Meditation is all Inclusive ~ Concentration is narrowing, exclusive'
Have a successful intention in the Universe. Dancing is Illegal now!
Sacred geometry; Don't fight really it's a prayer of devotional poets.
They don't get it, the vibe; People who can't take a compliment.
He was a Virgo. "Tell me you love me ~ Now!" "& forever!"
It doesn't matter anyway as long as I got breath in my body.

*

Extra Terrestrial Light
Natural Born Healer ~ "Looking is for free"
'Ugly is in the mind ~ of the beholder too'
We Are a Cosmic ship in Celestial Space

51

Please say nothing ~ Being Silence
Quantum science uses our 5 senses, nothing more, very limited!
It is and it isn't, the blind leading the blind ~ As it is as it isn't.
"I am the heart of the World and always have been"
The Great Central Sun which will go on forever ~ Om.
Try some contemplation ~ It's true it's not the full truth.

*

We want it; There is no they.
Holding up the maximum tempting carrot.
It's not Your poverty ~ We share everything.
Living in a squat, residing in a wrecked Renault Clio.
Projection of a victim, if you make that choice ~ your*self.
If you want Security, smoke Mary Jane by a Private Prison!

*

The Holy Goat
'Good morning Vietnam' *All on Acid past their limits!
And there's diseases that don't even have names yet ~
Lurking in the Liver river. The Illuminati took over God!
It's not about alright or not alright, that's only an opinion.
Everything is true and everything is false; It has no meaning.
Fancy Yoga patterns in time & space ~ sitting there dancing.
Don't get too happy, not gonna last! Creativity 'til you pass out!
Ask the people living in Kibera one of largest slums in Africa!
But we hang on desperately; Earth's Elites need a Revolution!
The Inequalities, Kings to paupers are too inhumanely extreme.
Reflections ~ no one to do anything, full Spontaneous Volition.
Who is Angry for nothing? No money to eat ~ Planet in Crisis!
Open eyes, closed eyes lives in a relative world take your pick.
"They've tried to Stop that ~ people being Happy on the dole!"
"It's well known, you never invite a priest around to babysit"

Star Fox Queen

"And those who were seen dancing were thought to be insane
by those who could not hear the music" ~ Friedrich Nietzsche.
Ultrasonic sound defying gravity. Hearing it live ~'Live & let live'
Simple, resonating with the Dalai Lama's concepts, Consciousness.
Stop differentiating; "The more you give ~ the more you receive"
'90% of people in American private jails are blacks or Latinos!'
Sweet apple of Creation; Need some simple SATISFACTION!
Psychedelics showing you ~ Opening you up.
Not about one time but being there all the time.
Self-suicidal Ego killed by Ram's Consciousness.
Sense that it has to go away ~ The C A U S E
*Being O N E * We Absorb * N A T U R E*
*

Thinking Senses.

What's the point of having a colony if you can't live there?
The Biggest lie, 'India the largest Democracy in the World!'
Can't afford dal, rice, onions, puri bhagi, Iodine sandwiches.
Live for good, for small things! 'Thin line between hope & dope'
Something as a concept, made into a metaphor ~ then...
"We want to see its structure" Bowing down to the Idols!
"I gave my soul for Rock & Roll ~ & yet I am still alive!"
#1, 40% of the World's Cocaine consumers are in USA'
How do we know what's in the toothpaste? Ask at A&E.
Western Philosophy tells you how to think ~ Mr. Big Brain;
Eastern philosophy how to Stop thinking! Surrendering, refrain.
They had studied thinking and found it to be too disturbing....
Lose your thoughts in Meditation ~ Mind is an asshole sometimes!
Isn't it dispiriting? 'Everything is good because you are there'
Not in a rush to enter Heaven not being given any choices.
'ENCOURAGE HUMAN FEELINGS'

Mind Healing Is Clarity

You are your Life ~ What's your incentive?
'A spoonful of sugar helps the medicine go down'
You're creating as you go ~ It's a FREE process.
"My motivation has never been about myself"
'Will I find a boyfriend?' Good luck tu yu numpty; Need more Information.
"They want you to tell everything" ~ without using their Divine attributes!

*

Life teaches everyone

Get yourself a Power tool! "Giving because you can"
Read the book with Intuition ~ then you'll get it.
Saying lots of things between the words ~ that's Art!
Reflecting it through the Heart ~ Being in the moment.
No separation, no individual entity, no such thing as YOU,
no more opinions ~ All the wheels of the mechanism turning.
You're going to have your epiphany; your head will be full of stars.
All the time being your own Satguru ~ Positioned right in front of the Sun.
Channeling Satsang ~ full of Light

*

Didn't shed any tears

She has entered the great Silence ~ It's Death!
"They don't exist anymore ~ it really is as it is."
'Let the dead bury the dead' ~ Is that a Response?
"Just wanted to get a gun and shoot him full of holes!"
You are the past projecting the holographic future ~
because of your memories reacting to pain or pleasure.
Home is where your heart is in the world.
Go with your feelings ~ with Awareness.
Be kind, share, don't anticipate & expect.
Fires of lascivious desire ~ A Head trip.

You Cannot Be A Poet And Not Feel

Only being in Time not out of Time ~ Coming together.
A Conscious Being praying to an Unconscious Object!
'God is the Very Life You Are' ~ 'Life Lives Life'
"There is No 'them' reinforcing the Illusion"
They're doing it....Who are they?
With a brain full of Information.
We're all One underneath ~
How did we get here?

*

Multi * Faceted ~ HAPPY YOGA

Superimposing whatever illusion they want on a virtual green screen.
All just labels we put on people; Hellfire missiles are very f....Real!
'YOU CAN STOP THE WAR ANYTIME' ~ YES WE ALL CAN.
'Yin*Yang, It'll either happen or it won't happen or neither or both'
Opportunities to Love, you're Not a Robotic, metadata machine!
Just another species with feelings thru your Cosmic heart chakra.

*

Wizards & Bangalore Totty

"I was talkin' to Lao Tzu last week about denial."
'You can watch the body of your enemy floating by ~
Focusing on stories of people who don't have intuition.
Dysfunctional patterns, Ego only talkin' about Yourself.
Controlling Cogs in a Swiss Grandfather clock.
Doesn't miss a beat ~ Only what's real is real!
You agree there is a New World Order?
There is No World mate! Letting it go.
States of Mind * changing all the time.
You have to see it as naturally divine
Magic ~ feeling that Life is amazing.
There's flowers all the way to the end.

None the Wiser

I should have given some Attention to Life ~
It's an inner feeling thing ~ not the dreaming.
"If you're waiting for me to leave, to feel your heart beat,
then one day I really will be gone from you" ~ Moving on.
Right mind is a tool to connect us ~ making us realise.
"It's fuckin' mesmerising, I've mesmerized myself!"
Not Thinking ~ being AWARE of your PRESENCE
*

It don't miss ~ Full Trippy.

Better be very quick, pesticides killing all the bees!
Anti-Neonicotinoid Army; Don't fuck with other people's honey!
Stirring his shallow pot ~ he's as spiritual as a brick.
"I can forgive not forget" "I'm not an opinion, I'm a friend!"
He wants that *SPOTLIGHT* always
trying to fill that hole of his loneliness.
"Once I've had enough I don't go back"
Cut off friendships, bye bye Sweetheart,
eventually feels good to let it all go ~
*

PSYCHE * ACTIVITY

Coke's sketchy, that was then this is now!
"Drugs don't really fuck me off, a good comedown"
If it's messy you know not to do it again ~
Trying to keep it together amidst lots of suffering.
"Are we really gonna have dead skin everywhere?"
If you're a Russian star here's a gram of MDMA!
Exploring the Totem of Taboos and Archetypes.
"I don't know ~ everybody's got a story"
"Hari Krishna, Hari Radha, Love & Light"
Being really happy with life

Synchronistic Fusion
Crystallization of being ~ coming directly from Observation.
Just there, watching life's movie, you're not the doer ~
Using all those songs to work through my own suicide!
Got a natural sociopath in charge of the camp!
"Get rid of that Opinion, you are the Maestro!"
'Anatta' such beautiful poetry in any tragedy!
There is no conspiracy, absolutely nothing ~
You are behind the watcher, actor, director.
All knowledge is there ~ Cosmic Virgin
metamorphosis oozing nectar in Paradise

*

Becoming Real
Raising your vibrations ~ coming out of her milky way.
Not taking the divine, sacred magic away.
Send a bunch of healing Angels ~
They're coming in waves ~
*'I Am * Goodness'*

*

Original * Archetype
Everything has to be In Space ~
that outside Space becoming One.
Please send that angel over here!
Download the juice from the others.
They take over your hands.
Came for a natural healing.

*

God as the Normal
Once upon a time ~ "Where else better to be than Goa?"
People with a big, demanding ambition can be disappointed.
"Even when I'm fucked up I'm happy!"
"You wanna be happy?" ~ "I am happy"

<u>L'Amato</u>
Like two ships passing in a night of Passion.
All memories not real ~ this is your bondage
so it can have what it wants ~ little kids do it!
"I'm a fallen star in her life, after making her
life completely Shine"
Use 'I' not the 'Me' ~ One thing leads to another.
The 'Me' is all lies because it wants things.
As It Is

*

<u>Moving Forward</u>
Winner & Loser; Flashes in the Pan*opticon.
'Our Employee of the Month's Free parking'
Awareness is the Fire that doesn't burn you up.
Passion ~ lust turns you into Omnificent dust.
We're always in touch with each other; Tag & chip!
Have to be in the Present ~ Not to have any opinion.
Integrating the understanding use your own Intuition.
Nothing in the box that her image is attached to ~
Respond with Love ~ who knows what people think?
What do I think? "I got my own life"

*

<u>Detoxing from Conception.</u>
Did they teach you ~ 'Inspiration' at les Beaux Arts?
PASSION about her work ~ Wonderfully in her heart.
"I'm not busy being born I'm busy dying"
"You see in my eyes how much I love you"
And still walked out the door with scorn on her cheeks.
Nothing is totally negative ~ Don't Panic mate!
We'll never destroy her nature, she is stronger.
Exuberant Magique ~ C'est plus que 'Moi'

<u>*"Who made me?" That's a very good question.*</u>
"I Am the Immeasurable frequency of Love ~"
Back in the Spiritual Universe with a Bona Fide Baba.
"It's man who made God into his own image"
"The last coup they had him under house arrest!"
The Scientists will catch them and fuck up their dimension.
Brainwashed us, dogmatic Priests controlling all this Theology!
"It's God who gave the apple to Eve and blamed some
imaginary serpent" ~ Ask even the (Activist) pilgrim.
Making the lustful, delicious Pagan Pan into a devil.
"SEX IS NOT A SIN" Thank Cosmic Eros for that!
We're all the offspring of our gorgeous Divinity.

*

<u>*It's all about the tone.*</u>
Cross over dimensions and suffer any consequences.
"Liberation from Yourself ~ not of yourself!"
Where is the juice, nature's Celestial nectar?
I see it from the heart ~ feeling that Love.
Go outside smoke a joint, look at the stars.
Everyone wants this golden alchemy.
Your beingness in the Sun

*

<u>*Quick tonight Kryptonite*</u>
'Alter Paraiso' and Ayhuascan Shamans in Peru.
Living outside time ~ she's dripping with jewels.
Touching God through your hair's divine energy.
You want trouble, drama, a Fukushima ghost in your life?
"I didn't get to the top of the food chain eating vegetables!"
Awareness sets everything alright ~ We are what we are.
Her Honey sweet Prasad is Best ~ Showing me full Love.
Our Cosmic Space ~ Our Cosmic Heart.

Tantric Hard Core Overdrive
Something to share ~ accessing a pure mind.
Keeping the Sacred Hologram spinning Alive!
Falling deeply in attraction to attachment,
fabulous chemistry in our unknown brains.
Your quantum particles * full attraction to mine.
Getting into romantic desires, powerful love lust.
Projections of your Ego onto Mind's I MAX screen.
Loving without the possession feeling is fantastic.
The Fear is gone ~ end of an Addiction * FREE.

*

A Non-Duality Masterpiece In Process
It's like 'Goodbye' to something that was never real.
"To be a person is to be asleep ~ Meaningless"
All just Ego bullshit with honour, take it easy, simply.
"You'll find out what sort of cunt you are with an opinion!"
"It all means nothing, get out ~ Hallo we're Responding!"
Don't react > being creative ~ CREATIVITY I AM US.
Not being in a lined box and only doing what you're told.
Not wrapped in gold balls of string making a knotted Ego!
Rat in the kitchen ~ "is just the pet!"

*

The Monkey Vibe
Divine Cosmic Acid, Moon Juice ~ Shiva turning blue!
Be in the moment, if you enjoy it be happy, don't waste
time worrying about what's on the other side of the wall.
Everything you do, delusions from your confused Ego
because it didn't want to pay attention ~ Surrendering.
Absolute Tao, Passionate about her work, if you have it use it.
Life teaches you, natural Spirit ~ "We're open to everybody"
Psyche*tropic not the Psychotic.

'Brain Washing 101'
"What was never lost can never be found"
Walked into a room full of Matisse's coloured light.
'Constant Predatory' ~ All just a concept Mein Fuhrer!
Always On Air, if you let it get you ~ it's gonna get you!
Paranoia on Top, try being a United Force.

*

"I love it man; Yeah I keel it!"
'One Nation's terrorist is another's freedom Activist' N'est pas?
'I don't wanna be around women who tell you to 'F… off'
Always welcome whenever you are ready.
Mind ~ is the Enemy; Calling the Babas!
Trans*parent Psy*Trance music, pure no disguise.
Cosmical, natural, everything bursting from light.

*

Finding Connection
'Left in middle of night, she's destroyed my Transcendental light!'
People want to take away from each moment because they
don't feel that Magic ~ resonating in Psychedelic Space.
You're Full lightness, no energy vampire can catch you!
From that anti-virus Consciousness becoming Awareness.
Long ago the Pharaohs asked the oracles for a description of
'Life in the Universe' try energetic space ~ We are unlimited.
Mind came to give limits ~ Mind is a conceptual Archenemy.
Wants no patterns, needing a Point from where to calculate.
Needs a Cosmic yardstick * we are the ones interconnected.
When we realise our enlightening Spirit ~ on the battlefield,
from mass carnage ~ got over Fears of Death & Suffering!
It's y/our own reality ~ Creation being here now absolutely.
We are * telepathy * I am a transmitter * You're a receiver.
Vice versa ~ No one knows what's goin' on, no idea ~ love it!
What's the example of your culture?

'I AM an Off * Planet Legal Alien'
'Archaic Church ~ Man controls his woman, his beast'
Scared to death of Sex, their Religion's rites & rituals.
You're a terrorist, racist, nationalist fascist, protagonist!
Dealing a Gilt trip. "Go and have the time of your life darling?"
"Lots of gorgeous women, a bit of what you fancy at a Roman orgy"
Changing fluorescent nylon Burkas for diaphanous Togas;
"Let's Av it!" ~ Calling for another f…. human sacrifice!
*

Purely chemically enhanced.
How you ever going to confuse Skunk with the real thing?
At a Cannibal Banquet ~ eating the ears & head, heart &
liver, android eyes & balls; Tongue & kidney pancakes.
Everything about Energy ~ receiving and transmitting.
"I'd like to keep us in this omnipresent Love frequency"
They seem to like to keep us in the Low, dense gravity.
They don't like it when your lasers are shimmering.
All together now, we are light * each of us * facets.
How much are you sending out? Try the sparerib!
*

Paying for that Freedom
To most of us it's unimaginable what they are transmitting!
TV; Algorithms, Formulae known to fuck us up for sure.
'Product for Sale' distractions ~ Drugs, sex, rock & roll.
What we are ready to receive ~ Now no masks, be pure.
Best way to take your own mind out of second guessing.
"If there was something else we'd all have been eaten!"
Trance figuration ~ direct connection to Consciousness.
'One initiated woman of power radiating divine heart ~
opening herself 'as love' can heal a whole community'
Sacred Union archetypes our Inner devotional imprint.
"I Love You"

Human Passionate feelings ~ different Mind
*Enjoy what you got * enjoy what you can get.*
'You can fulfill your dreams in surreal Goa'
Life force of the spark to lighting the fire.
'There's no power cuts in Chandigargh'
The Ape that ate the Magic mushroom!
Strong feelings of happiness and bliss.
Let's have 'em both.

*

*Freqs * of Nature.*
"We're always looking for what it is instead of feeling it"
"I can't believe how much Love is everywhere ~"
"This book, these words, will make you very wet!"
Put a fire under that chemistry, Ignite the bliss!
It is truly melting ~ in the burning out embers.
Hot coals smouldering away to Cosmic dust.
Nothing to keep the fire ~ going on empty.
Where do you start? Expelling it with light.
"Do what your heart tells you"

*

Above Thought Process
Enjoy the Ride, Chemistry flowing ~ accept them for who they are.
Not having any expectations and you won't have any broken heart!
Do it out the goodness of your heart ~ is the magic working nicely?
Catharsis, transformation healing go back to essential Pranic space.
Suffering breaks your ego ~ becoming very humble in the Cosmosis.
Peace of mind extracting out of your life all the difficult things ~
When you're at the top you know you can't go any higher until!
"There's a reason for everything even if you don't know what it is"
If it's pissing you off fuck it off. Understanding it the right way.
Don't look for it, feel it! She's five dimensional ~ Free to Feel.

<u>From the Plutonium Ray Generation</u>
Listening to a burning Atomic bush, "I am the Lord Your God!"
Intuitive Awareness ~Transcended the blind leading the blind.
Anyway it's the multi*dimensional river you want to be into ~
Why they don't wanna let the non-human Demon go?
Knots of Fear ~ Karma's out through the door!
The dream is not True ~ creative Imaginations.
You can talk about an elephant but that ain't it ~
The elephant's in the jungle being an elephant.
You have to decide with a Pure Heart.
It's all the same thing ~ you can find that river again.
*

<u>Rotary Bob</u>
Dancin' sweatin' the toxins away.
"I feel much better today!"
Joys of taboo * tattoo pain
"I wanna hear the drill rpm!"
"Oh I much prefer the silence"
"I want to be in love until I die"
'Live & Let Live ~ still that simple'
All the Freedom you have ~ to Love.
*

<u>Not Taking Sides ~ They're all off the wall!</u>
Tantric or DMT? They're both same Cosmic mystery!
Hysterical expectations ~ Allowing the Love chemistry.
He must have spent a lot of time staring in the mirror ~
A complete waste of energy ~ sometimes you can't avoid shit!
Taking courage to face the negative, do what the f... you like!
"I've got nothing on my mind when I wake up in the morning.
All clear ~ Reset for a new day"
"Ah I love happy endings man!"

Fully Unexpected Fatwa

Vulva's blossoming not shriveling up and dying!
All about the energy in dream ~ fecundity Vagina.
Who's judging your madness, stroking y/our egos?
Don't wanna be like them! Laws against natural weeds!
State of response, all Inclusive ~ Isn't Yoga exclusive?

*

Chakra Colours.

The World's perfect all the time ~
just unaware of it! Not you, with you the Space Opened up.
Freedom of Mind ~ living in intuitive, telepathic perception.
Heightened senses, Alert! Multi-functional wizards.
Crack Bombs in your Inner city playgrounds!
"Intuition isn't natural to the fearful soul"
Who's taking the Shuttle to Planet Oblivion?
"States of mind responsive not reactionary ~"

*

Fibonnaci's Breakfast

Patterns of Creation through different frequencies ~ colours, sounds.
Took up his role as 'Wisdom Keeper' Who wants a Happy Ending?
He'll give you a brain cell, putting in those missing links!
Non attachment to outside * existing as a free tree of life ~
Look at the spiraling Magnetic platform the pyramids are built on!
Red granite a breathing, electric cable connected to Solar energy.
Yin and Yang crossing duality*galaxy*spinning into a Cosmic disc.
Bio*energetic ley lines building it up ~ raising intrinsic capacity,
enlivening Stonehenge seeds, creative force for abundant harvests.
Universal concept ~ three dimensional space of the golden vortex.
Changing the frequency of a virus through Sacred geometry.
They all notice the firefly * You are the firefly!
Nature's electricity * Radiant Chi

Magnetic Pampers
Babies get pissed off quite a lot unless
they got a Big fat tit… Passion Myam!
Fillin' up me tank ~ on Love energy.
Cure ~ Hormones in your brain, do.
"You can't make that on a 3D printer!"
"We need to enjoy what is not what isn't"
Good to have Tantra alive in our hearts,
being here chanting beside sacred Tulsi.

*

Killer Torture!
Six months isn't a long time in the Universe * They have big
guns, weapons; there's no desire or passion. Here ~ Now!
'He was earning good money in Dubai then he went on
the Jihadi trip, grew a beard.' Inshallah Thunderstorms.
They gave him a doctorate and he's illiterate ~ Instinct!
It's all about Krishna's Love, everybody's happy smiles.
You are all that ~ you are the Cosmos.

*

Life can be a Jungle
"If you love each other ~ you idolise, being in adoration of each other"
'It's the acceptance of the mystery that's the answer to the mystery'
'Thoughts are ultimately expressed by love' ~ "I Love your Spirit"
Why would I want to deny bliss by not making love with you?
'You fill me with delight ~ only Brahma is Real.
The World is not real ~ the World is Brahma'
We have forgotten the art of communication, FEELING.
The dream self ~ where are your positive intentions
in our Conscious coitus fractal? Space for Meditation ~
'Feeling Reaction equanimously is the A W A R E N E S S'
Agoris and Naga Babas don't need SKYPE

Just won't get it together
He just gets up and leaves ~ Yeah many walk away.
Flash in a pan.. ain't nothing; She's a user, not real Baba,
she'll steal energy from you and anything else she Craves!
Everything works on balance ~ harmony is how it behaves.
Karmic lessons, heavy feet ~ change your ignorant attitude!
A different guise, "They don't do toast, don't do silence either"
She wanted, she wanted, something she thought she didn't get.
Your mother wasn't anyone, there is no Mother, just the Knower.

*

Another willing concubine
"I don't belong with sheep, I'm the wolf
and they have the right to keep me out!"
"I flowed like a river that's my Karma yoga"
You do it by being Absent ~ not attacking anyone.
'Your Life Is Your Life' ~ 'Innocent until proven guilty'
They're giving their Power away ~ to an Outside force. (I don't)
Powers making you learn, explaining,
educating all about your Free will!

*

Motivational Poetry
TOTALLY SURREAL DREAMING.
Part of the Healing ~ Be Inspired.
Feeling that deep depth deeply inside.
Becoming aware of it ~ transcendence
through Awareness ~ that's how it works!
'Self-enquiry' ~ Just look and it's for FREE.
People are having too much FUN for that.
OK the Party's over ~ "Where Am I?"
Numbers telling you to drop those Theatres.
"You can have as many lives as you want!"

Own Subliminals

Getting them in Your World.
Hypnotisng them with 'Salesmanship'
"Yeah I want that too, do you take Visa?"
By the time you get to the door ~
"What the fuck did I do that for?"
Autosuggestion ~ Here's my winning ticket!
Effecting the way you think – Monseigneur.
Implanted, voices coming out of the walls!
Have you seen the Mancunian Candidate?
Brainwashed but you're still feeling It!
Blushing in their facial expressions ~
Targeting your market with a Drone!

*

Things Yet to be Thought

"Is the Pope catholic… You'll never really know mate?"
Gotta make the most of it ~ Not getting smacked out
*of * R E A L I T Y ~ Every Mind so Beautiful.*
"Mind travels faster than light, ask a mammal"
*Switching it off to being here * now*
We're in this existence of the 5 senses
Getting into it! Experience the allowance ~
We create our own reality ~ really common.
Say it if you mean it not because it sounds cool.
"They're on but they're Not switched on!"
Gotta feel it ~ have to let it go, he can see;
'Through the Mind ~ Knowing and seeing it'
Watching making comparisons ~ 'I AM MYSELF'
The only truth there is even to a blind person ~
Can't be denied ~ Awareness of the whole thing.
'The World appears ~ the Self disappears'

If they so desire.
Who are You? Fuck have a nice day. Asking pointed questions.
Don't play politics, don't have a judgment, opinion, reaction.
Willful disobedience ~ "It's my Life" "Really, Fuck off!!!"
Don't I have the right to die on the street?
"I love you" ~ you feel what they do…
Don't want to see you die in front of me!
Love yourself ~ Keep it in your mind.
Rice farmers in the field are very Zen.

*

Cuddle Puddle
'Tres charmante' that rings a bell!
"You gotta go when the bell tolls"
That's what gongs are for ~ ding dong Yogini.
"Do you wanna try some DMT; It's Free?"
I let the Spaceship from Venus pass by ~
Catch that Cosmic trip on the next full moon.
Being flow ~ Karmas are patterns of the Mind.
If the always Sun's shining everything's all right.
I love the energy in a room of beautiful women ~
'I do what I do, I stand in my Truth' *Happy human.
Why would you slaughter, massacre your neighbour?
"I'm not regulated by what other people are Thinking"
It's not just a passion ~ It passes following your Star.
"That's what I want" ~ T R A N S F O R M A T I O N
Going to Infinite NO SPACE with all the chords detached ~
Source of Illusion ~ Observing Theatre, pantomime, Live Show.
Can't pretend I AM GOD, very nice, now go & do the dishes!
Your emotional body cleans out; No guilt this is who I Am.
Consciousness all at once ~ no time or space.
"Seeing it for what it is ~ then IT Stops spinning!"

Transformation for the better
Mars is dreaming in ~ this powerful, Cosmic radiation.
It's the Chemistry ~ how much can I afford to live with?
We can replenish our Aura ~ being within a Flame.
He was catatonic, we're living through Images.
Doing his duty with pleasure; We need Shakti.
Going with the flow, parking his mind, to be Self.
'Never mind the mind ~ you're always in the heart'
"Giving it your feeling, Stop thinking ~ Love me Now"
*

The Constitution really doesn't mean anything anymore!
The Role Models at the Top shown to be immoral, useless!
Aboriginal patterns expressing Songlines of the Universe.
Tuning in, resonating ~ they paint night skies full of stars.
Abstract art is about letting go ~ no 'Framings of Reference'
Creativity oozing from your fingertips ~ being in the moment.
Neutrino streams of molecules ~ flavours inside her Heaven.
*

"Given her a bone to chew on General!"
Aung San Suu Kyi ~ "If you're feeling helpless, help someone"
Tax on Tax on Tax on Tax ~ Fines, Penalty points, Oppression!
It all ended up in the coffers of the Vatican Luciferians!
Don't be Controlled by the agents of Demons.
Ruling things ~ telling you what to do!
*

Facing the Fact
"When I'm happier I'm happy"
"You'll get everything for Free!"
"You can't keep any secrets in Goa"
We should all have someone to Love.
It's accepting the change ~ inevitably.
Kohl burning inside her Shambala eyes.

Avant Garde Alternative

Abstract Art is about letting go ~ of Conventional.
Being original, creative, new, fresh counter culture.
Stopping the Thinking, parking the Mind for awhile.
Shakti using the Male as a tool, finding another host!
She'll go with the man who can give her what she wants the most.
Genes find the best provider to procreate ~ reproducing yourself!
All she's looking for; Press the right buttons & she'll believe it.
Polarity Dancers bathing in love and adoration, sucking it up ~
But she really loved me last night! Now sign the legal contract..

*

Rehab in a Fema camp

Ask me something really hard that I should have forgotten ~
Collecting the Revenues for Crime not about Class A drugs!
47% of 2.1 million US. prisoners are in jail for drug offences.
Busting all for a single little spliff! 'No holes barred!'
I gave him 2000 rupees to try to ease his identity pain,
not to insult him or to undermine his dignity with shame.
Taking his Dinosaur out for a walk ~ You gotta be You.
That's when I fell into the river ~ Squirt away!
"It's parallel ~ overlapping Universes isn't it?"
"I had a dream you bought me a ticket to Goa"
'Kundalini Syndrome' go and see Spirit Baba.
There's No one to change ~ reeds shaken by the wind.
It was Jesus by the way! Are you not always Happy?
Isn't it the natural inclination of the soul ~ naked in Paradise.
"I made you P e r f e c t ~ there's nothing to change!"
'OM NAMAH SHIVAYA ~ OM NAMAH SHIVAYA'
Being the moment ~ If you enjoy it, be a Happy sheep?
Don't waste time worrying about what's on the other
side of the electric fence!

Lucifer ~ Keep that dude down!
Alpha Female ~ soulful lady with the flying broom.
"I need a home for my suits" A Massive Projection!
Your life ~ have an alternative; "I don't own a suit"
Struggling to survive, you're Not free (In your mind-set) yet.
Mystical villages in the clouds ~ when I silence the voice.
"Just what Goa needs, more swimming pools!"
"I don't wanna be the Richest guy in the cemetery"
Power of believing in children, entering as a little child.
"I could see the frequency ~ hear Angels singing in my chest"
*Tantralising * Easy Tigress!*

*

Tantric Body Owner
'Not a spiritual monk but sharing my energy' ~ Reflecting yourself.
A dress is important outside, Inside is truly marvelous naked You!
"Killing is a holy thing getting rid of another f... infidel!" Hey man!
Virgins at the next corner all for you; Blow it up quick as you can!
Sexual energy directed at that Heaven; All those chicks
waiting for you, sooner you do it the faster you get there!
Insane ~ the more you kill the better entry into Paradise.
Very materialistic, Slave to the five senses, still in a cage!
Not free, you surrender ~ slave to supreme consciousness
From out of Bhakti devotional love ~ not forcing it on you.
That's beautiful!

*

Demonic Domestic Behaviour
Tuning to Vampires, 220 languages gone in years!
They pick it up fast ~ life is the biggest teacher of all.
Divine spiritual Universe ~ You're never coming back....
You've had materialist adventures; Bamyan up in smoke!
Programming starts at an early age ~ for many games.
You've Storm troopers killing Arabs ~ Videos on the net!

All Programmed to...
"The Hell of existence caught in Reaction ~"
Got no data to lose, choose another popular Program!
Controlling what we know & how is our Response.
Androids ~ totally Tamasik ~ Ayurvedic balances.
Trance Vedanta ~ "I didn't take any backshish!"
Do you remember her? She's your Soul mate.
Do You Think You Are In Love ~
If not why not? "I don't really know"
A perfect moment going with the flow.

*

Snowden's Revelations ~ Being Honest
'Mostly show an executive arm snatching exaggerated powers
with no public debate or parliamentary approval.' Democracy?
Dogs are more into Unconditional love ~ more enlightened…
I want to be a wo/man, a human, today whole World is enslaved.
'Not Personal only Spontaneous Volition' ~ What is Binding you?
Have to break the rule to see if it's a rule. You got a gorgeous body!
Your mind works only with opinions, have no judgments, it's Chaos.
What's goin' on up there? Once upon a time there was Pure water!
Corrupted by the Earth; what do you think, Tim Osman is dead?
No Rules ~ these people understand…. ask about the empathy.
Just be yourself ~ The Truth does set us all Free instantly.

*

Inconceivable to me
Why would you want to spend any time behaving like that?
Nature in the 10 to the power of minus 47 World of Reality.
Overlapping Parallel Universes ~ Isn't it? For gaining what?
Slums next to Palaces, is inhumanely criminal, wrong!
'People who are HAPPY in themselves want to make
other people HAPPY' ~ Foot pressed to the peddle!

Boys' Toys

Android * Robot * Real * Ideal * Lover.
SHE * Blissed out ~ her Amour fully Open.
Smiling, no ego, self-abandonment in Ecstasy!
You get the deeper reflections ~ deepest feelings.
"I don't want any more pain & suffering programs!"
Why F... would yu? Expendable, she's letting you go...
Gazing face to face, eyes to eyes ~ Pleasurific.
Tweaking them to the Max of beautific ~
to ring some (more) bliss feeling out of it!
"You don't wanna wait for that anymore"
Rude Boy Style ~ I do rudimentary channeling,
see that expression as an expression of your lust mate.
The Penis cult, big nipples, facials, welcome to the Orgy.
'Hari Krishna, Hari Krishna, Hari Rama, Hari Rama'

*

SWEET LOVE TANK

"I'm at home why not Stop by for another kiss?"
'Is it the right of the strong to oppress the weak?'
'Might Is Right' ~ then why didn't you just swallow it?
Who owns all the assets in a Ponzi game of Global Monopoly?
Time to Stop ~ no sense if you can't breathe! What'd yu think?
He's only thinking of licking a line off an Android's silicon face!

*

Banzai * FUK U SHAME * Hara-Kiri

"For a nation obsessed by saving face at all costs; TEPCO
must really be Mortified that THEY fucked the whole World!"
All the plankton is dying in toxic Oceans, all life forms ~ gone.
Even India is sending probes out to discover new life on Mars!
'Riding Kamikaze winds across the Pacific on a Plutonium reactor'
All the Dolphins are already being massacred in Taiji Bay, Japan!

"When She Shines She's Blinding"
"Get Married spend best part of your life only with your wife ~
or just fly to friendly Cambodia. You're with a Gorgeous person"
"She didn't say a word, put her arm round me, wiggled her bum ~
I didn't touch her or anything!" Just Looking for a bit of what yu fancy!
Not just about Cosmic sperms ~ blood's rushing to his vibrating Cock!
Always slipping down in-between a gorgeous, giggly Russian Sandwich.
That's what you dream of, can't be helped Baba, "I'm a dick on a stick!"
"I don't remember her face" ~ Sunbeams were moving around at night.
Lying there with her legs open ~ Flashing*Gone off like a Rocket!
Always being with a different incarnation of Maya Rati.
Rock & Roll, Bed & Breakfast ~ Happy days.
*

It's just about You ~ there is No other.
'Spiritual journey ~ suffering in the beginning becomes Joy'
"I'm a guy who got out" "We were always out of the Matrix Vibe!"
More you become now more you will be the Heart of the World.
"What am I afraid of?" Self-enquiry for the benefit of All.
You've lined up the 'You' 'I' and the 'Me' with mirrored
reflections which is Brahma for the benefit of All.
*

Bio*luminescent*Krill
'She does Love me ~ just not living together' Our Perception.
'Relationship is Relatedness' in the context, being here ~ now.
Can't turn that off, shadows of a Paranoia, Panorama Program!
You can do anything ~ the Divine can do; I'll prove it to you!
It's the 'ME' that's going crazy, you don't want that anyway.
"I choose to be a gentle Druid wizard picking meadow flowers"
"You're not the doer ~ let your mind go crazy by itself"
We live in a dimension of endless possibilities.
You want to be 'I AM'

Revelation of Your Sins

"Believe in me and I will fulfill your wishes & wash away ~
Not for that generation of men sent away to be slaughtered!
Left with a shattered, fearful psyche, full of severe Traumas.
Where is your sense of Sacredness? Overactive imagination;
Meaning ~ captured ~ Really what's life today all about?
He died at the muddy front line ~ rebirthing in Paradise.
Earthly or Celestial, ask at a field full of standing stones!

*

Real at the Garden Gate

Exotic ideas of enlightenment.
She became the lover of his life ~
Delusionally happy in the village.
Idealistic rainbows & thunderstorms.
He took his feelings & made a painting.
Then the failure, the rejection, loneliness ~
Impotence ~ 'hid her portrait under his bed.'
Disconnected, empty, passionless, doomed ~
from the start! Cold meat with no eye contact!

*

Dilettantism lad!

Heading to the dark, forbidding mines of Bolton.
Granddad down deep staring at a cold, coal face!
Survival of your genes digging their way forward.
'Letting the appearance tell you what's happening
not you imposing your will and Ideas on it.' AWARE ~
Didn't want any elegant fantasies, only Grim REALITY!
Is any of it socially relevant in this working class World?
His mother was a manic depressive prone to fits of violence.
Nature was Alive, in relationship * Sunrise, heading to the pit!
'WTF ~ he was a Surrealist before Surrealism was invented'

<u>'Slavery is a State of Mind'</u>
'Slavery is Not a state of mind' ~ Neti * Neti * Neti.
"You smoke these it'll help yur cough!" Wabi-Sabi.
They sent us to the Stars* she believes in Angels.
'As long as you make the best of your decision'
*

<u>Manifesting Metaphors</u>
"You gotta be able to lose it" ~ let it go into Space.
Always scared of something they can't control.
"They'll offer you a plate of fairy dust right away!"
Have you noticed not many white rabbits in the jungle?
Shiva's Valley ~ Its E N E R G E T I C S
has a lot to do with it * Psytrance frequencies!
"It's the Synergy Vibe!" Being Free * Synchronicity.
It's not who's got the biggest speakers but how it's in the flow!
'To be in it or not to be in it' ~ Ain't the answer to any question.
The one he's with now is the one he's with ~ being in this moment.
"Everything's coming from the Universe * There is no copyrighted!"
No.1, "She's so gorgeous & amazing I just wanna climb inside her!"
*

<u>Whirling Mental Trigger</u>
Mr. & Mrs. Jihadists; She couldn't drive the getaway car ~
so chosen to be the one for Holy Martyrdom in God's name!
Better get her a recycled Koran right away; kissing the gift of Allah.
When the Kaaba's stone turns completely black it's Judgment day!
"You don't get Alzheimer's because you already have it naturally
in your auras." Includes the schizophrenias and being senile et al.
"Senility is wasted on most people ~ how about 'fanaticism?'
Just alternative states of Consciousness"
And this tribe's creating exquisite psychic jewelry
flowing within Pachamama's flow ~

To embalm or not to embalm!
The white star is shining * above your Caravanserai door.
I am in bliss with your loving, Beautifully fertile, wet Oasis.
'Sexuality connects you with a frequency of ecstasy, which
connects you back to knowledge and to your divine source'
Feeling you tickling my spine*influencing my believed reality.
I accept your Invitation to surrender my love into your love ~
to let all the Oceans come together ~ In fecund anticipation
of a powerful thunderstorm on the horizon ~ deeply Inside.
I AM READY TO RECEIVE * A Celestial cornucopia
of Loving Perfection :)*Yes Please.
You are a shining galaxy in my life.
Sweet dreams ~ Sweeter dreams.
Her name means Gift of God.
*

PROPAGRANDAD
"Taj Mahal is mine ~ I can claim it as a Mughal descendent"
'Here is the formal statement I gave to Federal Police on
June 2012: On a trip to visit family in Seoul in April,
I was approached by a man and a woman who were Aliens'
I talked to him last night gave him an update....
he's not in touch with this reality....
That's ok I'm getting on with things....
There is a wonder*full life to live.
Here together ~ sunbeams and buttercups
clear light shining in the aura of their hearts.
YOU ARE MY INSPIRATION OF PASSION
It's everything you like ~ for free!

A war on Love, it's 21ˢᵗ century fascism!"
"How people survived the camps; God knows!"
'He couldn't speak but he'd always shake their hand ~
What are you hoping to gain by killing? Why're you so worried?
'We live not alone but chained to a creature of a different kingdom,
our body' & to Beauty & the Beasts of a different Planet * Our Mind.
When is enough, enough? For many, many, and many more people
there is never enough! And its effects on our lives and on the World!
Hell hath no fury as a woman who loved you, whom you loved, scorned.
_*_

*No Man's Land * Demilitarised Zones * No More Collateral Damages!
No more bloodbaths ~ realising these homicidal Wars are fully insane!!!
"Heretics hacked to death by 3 Suspected Jihadists who fled the scene!"
72,000 unidentified, allied soldiers left over from the battle of the Somme.
100th anniversary*Royal families on the memorial lawn having high tea
What's it say about our delusional establishments murdering you and all
yur mates? Really what have any of these chieftains achieved? Nothing
but horrendous death and destruction! More Noble sacrifices! 'Into the
Valley of death rode the 600.' "Where's my buttered scones batman?"
'Someone blunder'd. Theirs not to make reply, theirs not to reason why,
theirs but to do and die.' Who's funding miracles, who's editing the DNA?
Disconnect, let's all keep on Shining ~ It's very simple. 'At the rising sun
and at its going down we remember them.' Where's your son then dear?
Lost him on a foreign battlefield, slaughtered in a catastrophic massacre!
"There's my mum and dad laying a wreath of poppies at the wall of Love"
_*_

An Unconditional Eureka Moment
On the bridge of ecstatic blissfulness ~
Rumi ~ 'You are not a drop in the ocean
You are the entire ocean in a drop ~'
There is Love and there IS LOVE!
You Really Are

Re*energising Your Original*Blueprint

Goa very dreamy, 'Hanuman's a Winner!' Don't piss on my lingham!
Cellular It is as it is ~ it's not as it was, never will be again mate.
Nature's rivers don't flow in a straight line ~ ever-changing.
"I live with it every day, that's why I do what I do!"
"We gotta stick together otherwise we're lost!"
Remember when? I'm being in the happening.
I hope to be around at the end of Kali Yuga.
Beam me up Krishna ~ Miracles are real!
See them transforming in front of your eyes.

*

You Ate It

Nymphs in the pond "I'm not thinking of leaving the Planet yet!"
My next stop is swimming in the river Fuking it all ~ Cambodia.
They should be hung, drawn and quartered these Warmongers.
Evil fuckin' bastards seems to be all the Rulers for sure Baba!
Life is hangin' by a thread ~ Ask the Observer to please move.
An energetic carrier writing Love on water ~ crystal life patterns
Aligning in human, social harmony, resonating with the intention.
Conscious awareness not of anything just the Attention, feeling it.
*Doing it with the absence of thought*it's just this, whatever this is!*
Changing all the time ~ Mind focusing on Zen in a teacup.
'Damaged goods'....... "Someone will bring cake!"

*

Focal * Point

The brain is like a receiver for Consciousness.
What they don't care to Understand ~ life is being
*animated now*Consciousness lives, is alive in Space.*
*Can't see it, it's FORMLESS*thereby feel it In Yourself.*
*In Zero point * Stillness that's what Powers us*

Normally Insane

It's not what it is it's how it is ~ this moment in time.
Being conditioned by 'Rewarding and Punishment' ~
Forsaking now ~ for pleasure in an imaginary future
Shiva's seed ~ 'Heaven is a state of Consciousness'
It's all temporary life ~ "That's how we roll in India!"
"Don't store your treasures on Earth where they will perish & rust ~
*store them in Heaven where they will last forever" * Understanding*
*Space * We take it too seriously ~ "All the world is a stage"*
& we come to the end of the play!
Relinquishing the need to change and it
all changes by itself making everything become
Conscious and it works ~ Give it up, don't care,
transcending Dragon's Den, I play to Enjoy!
*

From what we have been led to believe

I am just this, really nothing to do here in the moment ~
It's the prison they know and won't let go of their Identification.
On Another Plane ~ 'If you're Conscious the money doesn't matter.'
2015/ '62 people have as much wealth as the poorest 3½ billion people
On the Planet!
*

Fiesta 1

"Always crashing in the same car ~"
See you in the next life.. Snuffed out!
You never know ~ tuning, resonating.
Living on that edge of not knowing
None of the suffering and pain ~
we give ourselves from the imaginary.
"Temporary existence means I will eventually lose
everything ~ meaning no attachment so no Fear..
*Consciousness existence is FORMLESS * Space.*

<u>Front Runner – Demanding a Stitch Up!</u>
Being on your own without needing anything ~ Feeling your Heart.
"I can't make You happy" ~ Don't project it, expect it of me darling!
Why do you want a rich businessman running the whole country mate?
When you feel like this inside you want to Share it as much as you can.
"She loves it when something goes wrong so she can Surrender"
Habitually criticising people, missing out on what it's all about!

*

ET 101. 'The Being-Human Manual' Reflected ~
Temptations at a Psychedelic Acid beach Shack.
Rocky-Fella wants them all micro-nano chipped.
Misleads people from the Truth then we're Fucked!
Feeling nature's ability to experience itself through us.
Celebrating the Infinite singularity of life

*

<u>Heart Pattern</u>
Fill that Space with Love ~
"All I know is that matter doesn't matter."
The supreme Brahma is seeing, is feeling ~
is hearing, is smelling, is tasting, is knowing.
Life of Consciousness
All Forms have that ~
Realising while we're all One.

*

<u>The Queen Cobra Cadillac</u>
Eating raw newts & she's covered in scars.
It's all becoming clearer in Phnom Penh...
The heart of darkness blazing up in flames!
Blessing the water going into the Wat ~
The river of a Thousand Linghams
it's in the Jungle

Listening to the Silence

Zen I am the consciousness for what's happening ~
Not being affected by gain or loss, playing of duality.
Life is not here to make you happy but transcendent.
Not missing it ~ Being fulfilled in consciousness.
Simply being present is the real freedom ~ Tao.
If you ever think you know, You don't know
Because Cosmic Space is beyond thought ~
Happening in y/our Consciousness
from the primal pangings of Space ~

*

Pure*Seeing

When you're looking at an Object with No judgment ~
When that Space is emptiness filled with Love & Compassion
Just being ~ Sat Chit Ananda.

*

Silence Is Stillness Inside

The psychedelic state is the one showing more the total aliveness!
Going beyond the conditioned, Controlled programming of the Mind ~
Ego using the apple, Adam in his tempted state eats the apple with Eve
*from the tree of knowledge of good * evil; Mind separating into duality.*
They see they're naked & feel ashamed,
told to leave Paradise, never to return!
Simple, perfect, natural environment ~ into the wild forests of Illusions!
*We learn to see the hallucinations*re-entering Cosmic Consciousness.*
Fell from Grace into the Ego within our DNA genetic information!
Narcissus falling in Love with his own reflection of Obsession.
Compassion for the Devil because
underneath we're all Angelic

The Ultimate <:> Idol of God
Mind can't comprehend the FORMLESSNESS ~ immortal.
Hell because it 'Matters' ~ not important but live breath is!
Totally insane seeing this conditioning state as normality.
"At war with the infidel again" Generation after generation!
You'll find out what's really inside me ~ Inside & outside
an Aware Space full of energetic Life*forces ~ SILENCE
Listening to the Nothingness ~ Attention & Awareness....
without any thought, respect; Stuck him on a cross to die!
If you're so unaware you don't know of your unawareness ~
*

Chimneys
The Chapora Chillum Massive!
Keep putting your feelers out ~
Sole existence makes you dance.
Into the exquisite ~ Petals of Love
*

Syrian Offshooting
It's gone beyond any fuckin' joke!!!!
"Is there still water alive in the Ocean?"
Lila ~ divine comedy, Jesus was a Bhakti.
*

Eugenic Signalling
Stopping learning through Education; Which, whose history?
Reading the environment ~ Who massacred the native?
'In America they've succeeded in bullshitting the people!'
Forked tongues, back doors into the dreamtime Matrix.
The 'Official' narrative, Dictators of the Men in Black.
'If you don't complain about anything
then you are giving your full consent..'
They want to Control this Whole World,
every Planet & Star in the Solar system!

Epiphanies for the Eye
Supercharged retinas and your peripheral vision ~
Duck! It's a drone XXX2269 cruising along the meridians.
Acid at the end of every pore of your skin ~ on its leys' cusp.
Every neural network is Energising in this vastness of Space
Feeling it all differently

*

Austerity Planning
People with a cow milking it and feeding themselves....
What they been doing in 1598 in the British countryside?
Went so many times round my head on that White Lightning!
Your body is capable ~ has the right to be here.
It's a Chemistry-set on the outside & Inside ~
'Fuck the Environment up that Fucks you up too!'

*

Hang on a bit!
You can see it with anyone who's been depressed.
Good question, 'when they gonna arrest the people
causing all this shit?' They're still walkin' around ~
counting their pounds under Government protection!
'The Mind Will Fuck You Up!' Try being Funky with it....
That's the mistake, we have a relationship with oneself
When We Are Oneself! Ask the Elk charmer..
***Pure Consciousness ~ One with Nature**.*

*

Musical ~ Shiva waves
"You choose your muse....
Interviews with a Geisha...
'The Importance of being Ernesto' or a Yoko...
"If there's no one to hear the music it's not music....
Died vilified, broken hearted on an inhuman treadmill

<u>Sinning in a dream of blissful Paradise</u>
You are the slaves of the Unconscious Mind ~ not living Peace!
Passion is Feeling; We're LOVE ~ be happy switch on empathy.
There is no blame game ~ ultimately everyone is responding
to 'PAIN' then it becomes impossible to bear any longer!
I had to let you go sweetheart and I couldn't tell you why.
We're all behaving with the same same craving, desire,
anger, grief, hate, disillusion of the swinging pendulum.
Do you want to create an Angel then make the Choice ~
To realise Compassion reigniting the flames of LOVE.

*

<u>Anjuna*Entertainment</u>
Dancing Full of Magic
'Welcome to the Asylum'
Amazed * watching it not in it ~
"She had the chance to finally act it out"
And I had the chance to witness her*soul.
Fully in it together*Feeling healing catharsis.
A Lover's exorcism ~ Conscious Expansion.
Lighting up her Unconscious deep black hole.
Fly like an Angel, I've given up ~ Pushing the Sun
Listening to dark chillum music! "You're more than welcome"

*

<u>Jam Packed</u>
They made all their money and their undetected getaway!
Open the closed blinds and let the light shine through ~
More people die from 'Selfies' than from shark attacks!
Why worry about parking the car when I'm going to die?
Negative experiences, they're a gift they'll wake you up!
Taking my attention from what's goin' on ~ disinformation.
*Cutting through the Illusions of the Ego states ~ It's **R**eal...*
Can't isolate it in Totality ~ Let's dance....

Devouring Puja Spores
They don't ask you to chant 'OM' they ask you to be
in the vibration ~ Enormous Power in Our Presence.
Invaded by 'ET Aliens' riding mythical armoured horses.
The Conquistadores murdered every one of them to get
to the fabled Golden Eldorado; being burnt by greed!
It's against all sacred natural laws to kill anything ~
Fly Solar Lingham missiles with DMT. phallic heads
not Ego-megalomaniacs' geneocide in God's name!
*

Gazing at the Kaaba's Black Stone
Floating in vales full of brilliant yellow buttercups.
Worshipping at the Altars of an 'Object from God!'
Try to explain that concept to a fundamental Fanatic.
Nothing to do with outside it's all going on inside ~
Feeling loving faeries dancing in a sunlit glade.
'I wandered lonely as a cloud...
in fields of golden daffodils'
*

Brothers & Sisters where we're all the same
"He who has Power to gather wisdom from a flower ~
and wake his heart in every hour to pleasant gratitude"
Don't lose sight of our eternal root in a digital X r*evolution.
Can't you do it without Knowing ~ Feeling we're all connected?
Dancing without knowing what is happening all around you ~ be.
Right or wrong perspective but defendants of their right to be right!
Killing sacred forests and Indians at a Pow-wow, ~ Fuck You no!
Being cut-down from any FEELING of LIFE.
Scream if you want

Without Limits We Are Stronger
Bank of England, Power, Money laundering for the Nazis, fascists et al.
Owned by a German financial Cartel, Corporate invasions ad infinitum;
Creating World Wars then supplying weapons and finance to all sides!
"He who Controls the money controls the World." Profits up, up, up!
Standard Oil of New Jersey; Tyrants selling petrol to the Luftwaffe.
Sinking our Global economy; Rock bottom with Terrifying Stukas!
'The Ju 87 made its combat debut in 1937 with the Luftwaffe's ~
Condor Legion during the Spanish Civil War.' "Achtung Guernica!"
*

'Still waters are deep'
More Psychedelics have landed!
You're in it for all the Moon ~
from within the inner core of the Earth
streaming with magma to its carnal mantle ~
Venus' man trap, Captivation, "I LOVED that!"
The greatest of addictions wouldn't let you go.
Swimming in my veins ~ Simmering alchemy
Different reality, energy * one with nature.
Everything is changing gotta let it flow ~
Not inflating my sense of ego.... I Know
*

Tranced Out
Compulsive ~ Hyperventilation, don't stop driving...
AWOL; Realistic might be dangerous, be aware of it.
Needing to change the Perception of things ~ Realise...
Chose to be the past, memories, not getting what I wanted..
Unsatisfied with my free will ~ not only embracing happiness.
Homer once said 'War is old men talkin' and young men dying'
Missing You In Action.

<u>Speed Dial *Temple App!</u>
Where's the dancing girls?
Go find the old camel factory ~
take a right, left and straight on..
Iris Novaclitolova is back in town.
Rumi is a master Sufi poet seer.
'Love in the ruins' "L'amour to the end!"
"There is never a 'No' to a child!"
FREE TO FEEL
*

<u>Sharing God's Tribute</u>
Sympathy for Angels*The King of good times
And they came as Conquerors, never good!
Daksha ~ giving devotion to your 'Master'
"How far do I walk for a bucket of water?"
Genetic imprint*the one with the Big Tika!
To know you're not alone, safe, a beautiful thing.
'The Angry Bull Technique' ~ steamed to death.
Paciferians ~ "I'm not into sharp nails...."
"Nothing wrong with a 4 inch needle!"
*

<u>Super Consciousness * Beyond All Controls</u>
Went on a trip * complete flip out of your Mind but super happy ~
She was gone beyond the Frontiers of her own Identity*Egoscape.
Taking you to other worlds, shamanic insights, you gotta ride it out!
Swimming in torrents of raw emotions*expansion seeming so Surreal.
Repressed memories came alive rising to the surface and dissolving ~
Living with people no separation only LOVE when dragons reappeared.
This is the crimson river of overdosing broken hearts and tears' destinies
Gargoyles perched on high ramparts scanning all the human turmoil...
Watching the rising of a new dawn, rainbow coloured comets shooting
through the glittering heavens*inside a multi*dimensional sanctuary.

^Invisible*Illusions^

There is no 'I' Nobody knows anything ~ Ego changing status.
Essence of Free - will being Alive in the Universe.
Sparkle, sparkle, sparkle * Stars are everywhere

*

Venus' Border

Instinctive Ego, No empathy, 'Out of Order!'
Talking to my crippled arm, blah, blah, blah.
Personality disorders of a poisonous Viper ~
Dealing with the delusions right in front of us!
What is Really? Ask Narcissus by the pool ~
*of sycophantic dreams. **"Please forgive me"***
To the one showing you a dysfunctional fig.

*

Simple Sane

'Dear Dalai Lama what is Love?'
'Love is the absence of Judgement.'
That's good a Lover who meditates ~ Uhmm!
She must have made some nice connections..
It's hard anywhere when you got nothing ~
There are billions living on less than $2 a day!
Better if they've already been to an Osho Centre.
"A cardboard box is good too, can always burn a box!"
They don't know about 'Giving way' in Maharashtra!
Enjoying each moment ~ Be Aware, having gratitude.
Nature is full of just 'weeds' that's its essential beauty.
Tolerance & grace, same same ~ unique difference *Life *Light

*

Reflection

Being Conscious in an ever ~ changing
Multi*dimensional energetic Cosmic Ocean
Compassionately * Instantaneously

*Oceania Sunrise * Sunset Reflections*
A bright Comet sonnet ~ Is that Who I AM?
See it know it being aware of it Live it feel it be
as we gaze into Narcissus' intoxicating mirror pool.
Transcending all delusions, illusions, hallucinations,
conditionings, Identities, desires, cravings, Ignorance,
selfish expectations, sultry eyes and warm loving embraces ~
emotions, beautiful romantic poems filling her heart to perfection.
Have to be centred in Solitary, Silent, Stillness, watching it unfold
ripples changing ~ becoming calmer on the placid lake of the Mind,
realising what it is to be Human in the World, in this natural Universe.
Forgiving ourselves, smile and live in tune with all the Cosmic energies.
To accept and to allow the Sun's rays to a*light each life force on Earth.
To be with the Angels
*

*'As-Salaam-Alaikum * Wa-Alaikum-Salaam'*
You really fucked me up Narcissistica ~ if you let it.
I was going blind... by her be Aware! "Baba Please,
I'm not an Indian I'm not used to being treated like shit!"
"Somewhere at a European border today a child has been
tear gassed." Caste out, the Angry wo/man ~ Please!
"Is she OK?"- "She's taking the medicine"
Being a wild, beautiful Shamanic Angel.
Weaving her lovely crystal bead necklace
Respect animals and all other life forms ~
Mother Earth of her own accord ~ let it vibe
To be calm ~ in becoming yourself.

Oily Fires blazing on Plastic Oceans

What the fuck can I do about Global warming, Black magic Psychopaths?
Earthquake, hurricanes, Super Volcanoes, Strontium 90 radioactive seas.
Powerful forces conjured up by others; Insane, criminally out of Control!
Why the fuck would you slaughter thousands of innocent Syrian people
and Dolphins in Taigi Bay? Nature you gotta Love it totally not murder it!
Drone bombs unexpectedly came from nowhere blowing up your house
family and school-mates; Today all inside were Collaterally obliterated!
Life is full of shit like this. What the Fuck they trying to get away with?
Has he been DNA. chemically diagnosed darling?
And who knows what really happened to her!
"It doesn't do to deny ones entire nature...."
Flood the box ~ Get a fuckin' grip!
*

*Love You Too * Tell the Truth, Who Cares?*

You are a sweet Angel, keep forever shining brightly darling!
'Europe's become too Commercial & desperate I don't like it!'
Reflex, 'don't look at him he'll want money or something else'
You already knew that hallucinatory pool of Full Narcissisms,
didn't you? Selfish Unawareness, deceitful that's how they are.
What was Judas? A liar, traitorous, treacherous, angry egoist,
jealous, murdererus, infidel, heretic, an apostolic wicked dick.
A anti-Semitic, aspergic, Narcissistic with passive-aggressive
X Syndromes combined with BPD; ASD; ADHD; Bi-Polarity?
Did he show any remorse, was he sorry, asking forgiveness?
A Lover's kiss of betrayal; tragically nailed himself to the cross ~
She's a knife-thrower >stuck it in his back & thru his heart & Soul!

It's a little Jewel

What a great line ~ taking it as it comes with Grace & Gratitude.
It really doesn't matter how they see it, how do you see it?
And she's put up with a load of shit for a very long time!
"What the fuck's it all about will someone please tell me?"
Off my head in a dazzling Sunburst
Limited time Un*limited*Infinite space
I'm not trying to construct anything ~
Caliente Cream Pies keeping my libido running on hot with Lily Love.
She's a cocksucking aphrodisiac, Smile Inside. Who wants safe sex!
Power of the pussy, "can I lick your vagina?" "Thanks for asking."

*

Kakistocratic Porn Starfields*Spread her legs go through the tunnel.
"I'd vote for Sean Penn to be President and Jennifer White first lady.
She destroyed ALL the sexual taboos in the VIP. room for us to see!
Opened up every hole for her black dudes crew to invade and ravish.
Looking for a woman with Big tits & a deep throat Bermudan sloop.
I gave the poorest girl on the Planet the nicest fuck & paid her $25.
My very own light Star shooting across her glistening Milky way ~
dripping down her mouth, with sparkling eyes craving a full facial.
Shamanic warriors in the disguise of travellers from PDR. Congo!
Do you want to be a Light worker, Victim, Martyr? Absorbing it all
Knowing with joy; You need to reflect from deep Inside your heart.
You either have it or you don't have it, fully attractive temptations.
Instincts of desire & Inspiration, it is what it is, isn't it of course?
Real Brain washed, talkin' to himself.... just let it all come out

*

God Is
Great
Dividing & Conquering ~
heretics naked on the beach
Making Love in the Sun

'Fall in Love with the person who enjoys your madness
not the boring one who forces you to be normal'
Isn't there a blissful in-between state somewhere?
I suppose the key words are falling in Love altho' some argue it should
be growing in Love. However Love is the Magic and while this chemistry
is vitally alive then amazing things do happen between those in that state
even tho' sometimes we may be blissfully unaware of why Force is never
good for Love although surprisingly people accept it in their relation*ships.
Love Magic is a divine lightness of being which is essentially free,
therefore such love moves like the stars and we cannot always
hold it in our hearts as much as one desires****;)))
*

"I'm on my way to Qolomango!"
'You have to read between the lines' ~ it's what's not said...
*

EARTH

BIRTH

MOTHER
*

Jasmine * Imagination * Inspirational * Illuminates
I* Illusion* Identity*the basis of all Mindkind's suffering.
'One does not become enlightened by imagining figures of
light, but by making the darkness conscious.'- Carl Jung.
How deep and how long do you want to keep rolling in it?
Composing silent Japanese haikus at dawn in a snow storm.
Crystal flakes float, Shakuhachi notes glide on the clear wind.
Can't we diagnose cancers in your horoscopes, in your Stars?
How can we know what makes a moment Ultimately what it is?
Infinity is running through all our veins ~ be in tune with nature.

'Why is Shiva Valley the Temple of Trance?' > Nataraj in Despair!
To maintain the unique energy of a place people usually abide by the customs for example, taking your shoes off before entering a temple or mosque, being silent, wearing a shawl ~ We are taught these as forms of respect especially as foreigners and thereby we enter into the correct spirit of the place. Women are admonished for wearing bikinis on the beach whereas it's accepted as standard by the Goa Government, to bathe in a sari! Obviously when the Goa tourism industry is selling expensive, long distance beach holidays to modern international tourists it should probably reconsider these directives if it wants to continue to successfully compete in a highly competitive world as it is suddenly realising by the loss of tourists! Sexually frustrated young and old men come from all over India and locally to experience new senses of freedom which they desperately crave in this changing Indian cultural, MTV paradigm which has been available to other cultures fifty years ago! They come to Goa which is not a dry state mainly to drink, take other drugs and so feel less inhibited. And they want to participate in other sordid activities which have put off foreign women from feeling safe and from even wanting to come to Goa as is well reported in all studies on Goa tourism and by the lack of female visitors! Uncle parties, stag parties of groups of 20+ drunken males rolling in one after the other all night long! An invasion of people who do not belong in Trance parties and only come to gawk, some even bringing their family and children with no interest in what is really happening in these places. They have no idea of the culture of the music, the dance, the vital energy that is being created by people who have made Goa an International Trance scene that is recognised by the music world and which is essential to the Goa vibe which is the Magic, why we are all here and loving it; Originating with the hippies in the 60's.

These people have been welcomed and they have treated the place with no such respect and consequently this energy is 'DYING' as fewer and fewer true believers bother to even turn up any more knowing that if it's not the Police closing the party down at 10 pm then it's bunches of Indian men acting with juvenile delinquent behavior trying to impress their mates from some town in India where they have been fed this image of a Free Goa where they think they can grab foreign girls and go on the rampage and be let loose to bother everyone else at the party with their rowdiness, talking, standing never dancing to the music, being in the trance vibe but instead posing, taking 'Selfies' for friends or the office or school! This is their chance to escape from the control, restrictions of their family and home. They would not behave like this there so why behave like this in our home and Temple? In the past ten years the Goa Government as shown in films, Documentaries such as 'Last Hippie Standing' and the 'diatribe' press has been vehement that it never wanted Goa Trance music parties. They had no interest in protecting these roots, they are more interested in the commercial mass Tourist and Alcohol business and their Heritage of making as much money as possible without any dynamic cultural development. Look at the negative Tourism impact studies. Realise it's now time to wake up and respect Goa Psy*Trance!

*

Imagination * Producing Belief
The Controllers want to manifest their version of Reality.
Spiral Esotericisms have you lost the Magicness of Life?
Is there any potential left in the Planetary Human Psyche?
Conglomerates by the bucket load; dark Vatican's wealth!
Uber Psychological Warfare, Cartels' Globalism Agendas.
Who is promoting the Genocide, massacres, slavery,
extreme inequalities, poverty, debt, disease, poisons?
Oligarchs what esoteric secrets do they really know?
Ask Prince Tallano where is Yamashita's treasure?
It can't be Human destiny whatever it is! RIGHT?

Akhenaton Extravaganza
'And what about Truth in the heart of a beholder?'
"Trust us this is not what the Universe wants!"
Who wrote 'The secrets of the Exodus'?
Sacred geometry & Psyche conscious poetry.
Research the Hominids' DNA; they'll tell you
there's more Gold than you'll ever know about!
It's in the IQ stored in the left side of their brain.
Preying on human impulses; we buy it as Ultimate reality!
Super Matrix computers, no emotions! "Do I know you?"
NOT A PRISON of DECEPTION ~ BEING OPEN
Imperceptibly delicate, sublime, changing streams
of loving devotion, blissful feelings that's you & me.

*

Discovering Truth's Expression ~ Until Lost
The Physical Universe is a Production of the 'Mind' ~
Transcending its Amnesia, how many Levels are there?
REVOLUTION AGAINST THIS TYRANNICAL EMPIRE!
Hypnotised the cultures, diluting the seas of Individuality ~
You're in a labyrinth of Mass control Not FREE Imagination.
Meant to deceive you, keeping their Power; send 'em to the Front!
Melting us down making us believe it is where the Sprit truly exists.
Don't we all want Peace, equality, happiness, security, no suffering?
Join into Bhakti, 'Satyagraha' 'SEVA' Selfless service, a way forward
for 7 billion plus people on our turbulent Planet, ruined by Psychopaths!
Don't believe me check it out for yourself. Half the entire population are
existing on less than $1 a day; 62 people have half of the World's wealth.
Check out who are the richest Oligarchs on Earth and the destruction of
Our environment & of other species for the purpose of Power and greed!
Time for a redistribution of Resources ~ sharing, caring for Pachamama.
Ask your Conscious & if you can't find it start developing being one now.

Dreaming of Venus
Her iconic naked body, her sexuality, purely sensual ~
She's offering a Beautiful Celebratory experience of Life.
Excitement, no shame, the most sublime, innocent bliss.
Blameless there is no sin ~ You can't diminish her Spirit!
She is the most desirable creature in the Universe

*

Venus Sans Retour
'Beauty is a distraction of God' ~ now who said that Aphrodite?
Where is our Goddess of Love? Floating naked on a seashell.
Once upon a time relegated to the deepest cave for bewitching us.
The face of the alluring female inspiring tenderness not lust.
I took her by the hand for our journey to the bridal suite ~
Sunset to sunrise sharing in sublime ecstasis * divine sex.
Priapus, Bacchus and the Queens of summer came for tea.

*

Nefertiti not a Human Genome
From their nuclear bunkers they will wipe-out the whole World!
Trusting my own Intuition not listening to any Puppet Masters ~
Whose are those elongated skulls Moses? Ask Homo Capensis.
Working for All of Humanity not for their Matrix of lies ~
Your eyes show lots of wonderful adventures to come.
Seeing Celestial stars in your Orbits not EET attacks!
"I was there to represent Reality working thru Space"
Deciphering souls hearing stuff in their heads 24/7.
Dividing & Conquering; who hijacked the Sacred?
"Why did you let the demon come out?"
Keeping us Forever Enslaved.
"I always hated bullies!"

Moon * Goddess
'Pagan nude ~ paintings are under attack!'
Rediscovered in the lost collection of Homer's Hymns.
Gave Rose bouquets to Venus in her garden of Nymphs
Opening jeweled boxes of psychedelics and aphrodisiacs.
Full frontal nakedness of a Goddess ~ driving us all mad!
'She was renowned for being the greatest beauty of her age'
*

General Inquisitor's Extra Horror
Matrix creators manipulating Reality ~ Conspiracy.
Bankrupting, dividing nations, alienating its people.
Mind-control from the Media, Entertainment Industry,
News, Lottery jackpot, a million violent Crime CSI. dramas!
Our individual energy is inside not externally happening to you ~
Compart-mentalised, given you a Flat-screen by the Image makers.
No real humanity, degrading, I think I'll go and live in Auroville.
*"I can see her emotions" * It's happening to YOU*
*

Sensational D'anger
Richard Dadd ~ *The Fairy Feller's Masterstroke*
Human Inspiration is everywhere*smell Frangipani..
'Had an incredible chance encounter with a troupe of
wild Mountain Gorillas in Uganda ~ gave me a hug!
It's everyone's dream today & why wouldn't it be?
Sent to a debutante's Charm school in Switzerland.
Taught me how to lie tantalisingly on a sun bed.
Voluptuously at a Romanesque banquet or out
in the cold snow pushing a horse and plough!
The Italians got style, they got more than style.
Brits' have an ironic sense of humour...
Sit back & enjoy a really brilliant fuck!

<u>*"Don't worry about me"*</u>
"When people say that...
they mean the opposite."
'He didn't care about money
He cared about people'
'America's most famous Muslim
Remaining true to the cause ~'
Vindication not forked tongues!
"He decided to be better not bitter"
*

<u>*"With this stolen car that he lent me"*</u>
Criminalising our wounded war veterans!
Glaring holes in the Matrix mythology net ~
follow these contradictions to clearly realise
what is right, what is wrong, what is ridiculous
what is violence gone mad, what is natural law.
'Do unto others as you would have done unto you'
Being naked seeing your true reality*natural beauty.
*

<u>*Schedule 1 drug - EEG Mind Control*</u>
Here comes CIA. Central Command, CENCOM & Vatican!
Give them a truth serum and ask them about Schizophrenia.
Is it for the Combat infantry or Anti counter-culture therapy?
'The Bank cartels own 40% net worth of the 43,000 companies
traded on Capital markets And 60% of their earnings!' Ask @
KarenHudes about IBRD; International Bank of Reconstruction
& Development + the International Bank of Settlements in Basel!
I got a micro-waved signal; Where does Inhuman*Madness End?
"If you don't stand for the Truth you will fall for anything."

<u>Open ~ Source</u>
An artist with a mental illness ~
Gone out of his mind on fairy dust!
Talking to the blissful Moon of faies
Dancing with the Elves in Trifle City."I don't give a fuck!" He said....
'The phrase "speaks with a forked tongue" means to say one thing and
mean another or, to be hypocritical, or act in a duplicitous manner...'

*

<u>Sex*drugs*Psy*trance</u>
"This is very nice; Keep it away from me!"
Party ~ like when the Freak family is there!
He's a brother from another Planet...
Brain dead at the end of night
"I'm not hurting anyone, I gave them both
a complimentary bag of crack & smack!"
Out of sight out of mind.
To tell yourself the Truth
How to cope with life ~
Looking at the other side of
the mountain ~ it looks different
that's what life's all about.....
Spread the Love

*

<u>FLASH * FORWARD</u>
Sometimes we have to go thru Hell.. I don't agree with that idea of living
the pain to get the gain; What do I know? Life can be like that**for many
don't deserve it 100%. Other people who we have a deep bonding with
can make our lives wonderful or a living hell, some say they don't know
any better; Why? Ultimately does that help you get through it without a
broken heart and more? You'll survive or you won't ~ another piece of
REVELATION appreciation. Sometime later Spring has blossomed and
Summer skies are shining full of light in her hair.

What Is Real?
"That's the way it is ~ it'll only happen if you're together,
if you're somewhere else you're somewhere else"
Let Divine take care of it, the expanding Universe ~ Where?
Monstrous revelation - Debt; Well I guess you gotta starve then!
Sinking back into the slithery slime of our primordial nature.
How do they behave, Illuminati they have no human empathy?
It's just about him there is no everybody! Negative, Empty.
Recognising his own Ego's full reflection ~
'Life Is Living Life'
*

Rishi Sikhedelic Turbans
Osho, "It's not a question of being in Love with someone ~
It's a question of being Love" Even the lumpy ones are alright, ask
Lingham Baba! 'Sharing in the energy of the feeling of joy radiating
from someone in Love' ~ "Love yourself enough to be yourself"
Don't expect any mercy, get on with it. Hippies are not trying to
change the world ~ it's always a good time to be in the garden.
*

Shattering Images ~ Love ~ Life Changes ~ Nothing lasts Forever
"I loved her fantastically now that love has disappeared forever ~"
"No, Love is everywhere, the Love's inside you" ~ Omnipresence!
No duality ~ it's within us, going on to Infinity *I Am Buddha nature.
Underlying emotions of Love ~ Deny yourself nothing; Consciously.
Tuning into changing feelings; You are Love, Cosmic Love Ocean.
Enhancing the clarity of its manifestation ~ reflections together.
It's not about in Love or not in Love or hate and disappointment,
attached, detached, connected, disconnected, conditioned or not.
There is no leaving her behind, letting her go ~ All being Love's flow.
Transcending the dramas, addictions, fully into Love's Omniscience
'May all beings recognise the fact that they Are all to be HAPPY'
And we'll all live happily ever after * SHARING * LOVE telepathy

ABOUT SUNNY JETSUN

Inspired by the sixties Sunny started traveling the world in 1970.
His spiritual journey on the hippie trail to India took him through
San Francisco, Los Angeles, London, Amsterdam, Paris, Vancouver,
Sidney and Kathmandu to Varanasi. His arrival on the sub-continent was
the beginning of writing autobiographical verses capturing his travel
experiences, encounters with remarkable people and his quest for self-
realization. Combining experimentation with drugs, sex, rock & roll ~
meditation, Love and life in general. Sunny started to open up to a multi-
dimensional Universe. He lived the mantra, "Turn on, tune in, drop out"
realising Mind's-illusions, inspired by deeper feelings of holistic nature,
empathy, energy * Space ~

Over four decades Sunny has written and published 28 books of poetry,
created over one hundred paintings, traveled the World and considers
his masterpiece to be his daughter. He has spent the past fifteen years
in Goa, India inspired by the freedom to experience and idealism of
human consciousness.

Sunny Jetsun books and art are available on the web at:

Website: www.sunnyjetsun.com
Facebook: www.facebook.com/sunnyjetsun
Amazon: www.amazon.com/author/sunnyjetsun
Smashwords: www.smashwords.com/profile/view/sunnyjetsun

www.ingramcontent.com/pod-product-compliance
Lightning Source LLC
Chambersburg PA
CBHW020509030426
42337CB00011B/301